Using
Photoshop
CS6

Robert Penfold

Bernard Babani (publishing) Ltd
The Grampians
Shepherds Bush Road
London W6 7NF
England

www.babanibooks.com

Please note

Although every care has been taken with the production of this book to ensure that all information is correct at the time of writing and that any projects, designs, modifications and/or programs, etc., contained herewith, operate in a correct and safe manner and also that any components specified are normally available in Great Britain, the Publisher and Author do not accept responsibility in any way for the failure (including fault in design) of any projects, design, modification or program to work correctly or to cause damage to any equipment that it may be connected to or used in conjunction with, or in respect of any other damage or injury that may be caused, nor do the Publishers accept responsibility in any way for the failure to obtain specified components.

Notice is also given that if any equipment that is still under warranty is modified in any way or used or connected with home-built equipment then that warranty may be void.

First Published - November 2012

British Library Cataloguing in Publication Data
A catalogue record for this book is available from the British Library

ISBN: 978 0 85934 737 2

Cover Design by Gregor Arthur
Printed and bound in Great Britain for Bernard Babani (publishing) Ltd

Preface

Digital photography was for many years "just around the corner". Digital cameras were always going to be the runaway success of the next Christmas, but for some years it never quite happened. With hindsight it is easy to see that the early digital cameras were too low in specification and high in cost, and were never going to be a mass marketing success. Some of us began to wonder if high quality and affordable digital cameras would ever appear in the shops.

Things have changed in recent years though, and it is now possible to obtain inexpensive digital cameras that are capable of producing large prints of high quality. Even some sophisticated digital SLRs and compact system cameras can be purchased at reasonable prices, and a high specification no longer requires an outlay of thousands of pounds. These cameras can be used in a very simple manner if preferred, with the memory card containing the pictures being taken to a photo processing shop in much the same way that a film is taken for processing and printing. However, digital imaging gives the photographer far more control than is possible with film photography, enabling huge improvements to be made to photographs after they have been taken. If photographs do not come out as you expected, it is no longer necessary to just "grin and bear it".

Of course, in order to fully exploit digital photography it is necessary to have a computer running a suitable image editing program. Photoshop has for some years been the most popular software for professional and dedicated amateur photographers. It is a program that is definitely not in the budget category, but it has a huge range of facilities that enable images to be manipulated and improved in just about any way imaginable. One of the main reasons for its success is the well thought out user interface that makes it reasonably straightforward to use. Anyone familiar with the basics of using computers and modern software should have no difficulty in using Photoshop to do some simple tasks. On the other hand, learning to use Photoshop really proficiently takes time and effort, and some aspects of photo editing require skills that can only be obtained through experience.

This book will not turn you into an instant Photoshop expert, but it does explain in simple terms how to use the latest version of Photoshop, CS6 to optimise image quality and how to exploit its creative potential. The emphasis is on the everyday editing tasks that will need to be performed routinely in order to optimise your photographs. The topics covered include correcting colour casts and exposure problems, sharpening "soft" images, adding special effects, undertaking basic retouching, cropping images, correcting distortions of various types, removing purple fringing, and providing redeye reduction. No previous knowledge of digital photography is assumed, but it is assumed that the reader knows the fundamentals of using a computer running a modern Windows operating system.

Robert Penfold

PC and Macintosh

Photoshop is available in Windows PC and Macintosh versions. The PC version was used in the production of this book, but in use there is very little difference between the two. The differences are mainly brought about by the use of different conventions in the way the two types of computer are used, and by differences in the nomenclature used in menus. Provided you are reasonably fluent in the use of a Macintosh computer you should have little difficulty following the methods described in this book. Even if you use the PC version you will still need to know the fundamentals of using the computer, but with either version you do not need to be a computer expert.

Trademarks

Adobe Photoshop and Photoshop Elements are either trademarks or registered trademarks of Adobe Systems Inc. Microsoft, Windows, Windows XP, Windows Vista and Windows 7 are either registered trademarks or trademarks of Microsoft Corporation.

All other brand and product names used in this book are recognised trademarks, or registered trademarks of their respective companies. There is no intent to use any trademarks generically and readers should investigate ownership of a trademark before using it for any purpose.

Contents

3

Selections and Layers 115

4

Adobe Camera RAW 173

Index 183

Photoshop CS6 Toolbar (Toolbox)

Move tool

Rectangular, elliptical and single row/column marquee tools

Lasso tool/polygonal lasso tool/magnetic lasso tool

Quick selection tool/magic wand tool

Crop tool/perspective crop tool/slice tool/slice select tool

Eyedropper tool/ruler tool/note tool/color sampler tool

Healing, patch and red-eye tools/content aware move tool

Brush tool/pencil tool/color replacement tool/mixer brush tool

Clone stamp tool/pattern stamp tool

History brush tool/art history brush tool

Eraser tool/background eraser tool/magic eraser tool

Pant bucket tool/gradient tool

Blur tool/sharpen tool/smudge tool

Burn tool/dodge tool/sponge tool

Pen and freeform pen tools/Anchor tools/convert point tool

Horizontal and vertical type/mask tools

Path selection tool/direct selection tool

Line/rectangle/rounded rectangle/ellipse/polygon/custom shape

Hand tool /rotate view tool

Zoom tool

Switch foreground/background colours

Foreground/background colours

Edit in quick mask mode

Screen modes

N.B. Right-click triangle in bottom right-hand corner of button for pop-up menu of other functions.

Adobe Bridge

Browsing

Photoshop has the usual facilities for browsing folders and locating files which can then be opened in the program. It can also be used in conjunction with Windows Explorer, which should include an Open With option for Photoshop if you right-click the entry for a Photoshop compatible image file. Depending on the way you like to work, these facilities might be all that you need.

However, there are two additional features of Photoshop that should not be overlooked, and these can make it much easier to locate and load the files you need. These are called Adobe Bridge, and Mini Bridge. Adobe Bridge is actually a separate program that can be run entirely independently or called up from within Photoshop (File-Browse in Bridge).

Fig.1.1 The Adobe Bridge screen is divided vertically into three panes

Fig1.2 Using the Folders panel it is possible to browse the image files present in any folder

Mini Bridge is used from within Photoshop (Browse in Mini Bridge), but it requires Adobe Bridge to be running in the background.

Adobe Bridge

We will start with Adobe Bridge. Launching it, from within Photoshop or separately, produces an initial window like the one in Figure 1.1. The screen has the usual menu bars and so on along the top, with the rest divided into three panes. The large one in the middle is used to display thumbnails of images, while the panes on either side allow images to be managed and displayed in various ways. The side panes are subdivided into panels, and some of these are in turn subdivided by tabs which enable a panel to be switched from one function to another.

Folders and Favorites

The top left-hand panel has tabs that enable Favorites or Folders to be selected. Folders, as one would probably expect, provides access to the drives and folders available on the computer. Selecting a folder that contains Photoshop compatible image files will result in those files being shown as thumbnails in the central pane (Figure 1.2). Note that, unlike

Fig.1.3 It is possible to make the preview panel larger

many file browsers, compatible RAW files will be shown as thumbnails and not simply as icons.

The Favorites panel displays a list of folders that you have designated as favourites so that they can be accessed quickly and easily. This panel will show some default folders initially, but you can remove any that you do not wish to keep as favourites by right-clicking them and selecting Remove from Favorites from the pop-up menu. Of course, this just removes the folders from the Favorites panel and they remain in place on the disc drive.

A folder can be added to the Favorites panel by first using the Folders panel to locate the folder and show the folder in the main pane. It is not the contents of the folder that must be displayed, but the unopened folder. Switch back to the Favorites panel and then drag the folder to the unoccupied area at the bottom of the panel. Alternatively, while still in the Folders panel you can right-click a folder and select Add to Favorites from the pop-up menu. Another method is to select the folder by left-clicking it, and then choose Add to Favorites from the File menu (File-Add to Favorites). With any method of adding favourites you can select several folders using the normal Windows methods of multiple file/folder selection, and then add them en masse.

Fig.1.4 It is possible to preview two or more images

Preview

The Preview panel displays a larger version of the currently selected image than the thumbnail in the main panel, although in most cases it will still be a tiny fraction of the full-size image. However, you can drag the dividing line between panes to alter their size, and the preview window can be made larger (Figure 1.3). The preview image is still likely to be very small compared to the full image, but an increase in size can still be very helpful. It is possible to preview two or more by using the normal Windows methods of multiple selection, but for this to be useful it will almost certainly be necessary to increase the size of the preview window (Figure 1.4).

There is a slider control near the bottom right-hand corner of the window, and this can be used to increase or reduce the size of the thumbnails. In Figure 1.5 the thumbnails have been made substantially larger. The problem with doing this is that the main panel can only show a small number of thumbnails, and may only be able to accommodate about half a dozen if they are made very large. Using very small thumbnails enables a large number to be displayed simultaneously, but each one might show so little detail that it becomes of limited value. The size setting therefore has to be something of a compromise.

Fig.1.5 The size of the thumbnails can be changed

Placing the pointer over a preview image results in the pointer changing to a version of the Zoom tool. Left clicking on the preview image results in a small window appearing, and this shows a highly magnified version of the image. This window can be seen on the preview image in Figure 1.5. I presume it is showing a small area of the image in Actual Pixels form. This "loupe" window can be dragged using the mouse, and it can therefore be used to display the desired part of the image.

Filtering

The filtering panel can be used to limit the images displayed in the main panel to only those that match certain criteria. This panel is dynamic, which simply means that the types of filtering offered will change to match the data types available for the images in the current folder. The filter categories will typically include such things as the date the image was created or last modified, the lens used, the taking aperture, focal length used, shutter time, and keywords.

Any category that is not relevant to the images in the current folder will not be included. For example, it is possible to rate pictures by selecting them and then choosing the appropriate star rating from the Label menu, but if you do not bother to rate pictures there will be no Ratings category. If you rate even a single picture in the current folder, then the Ratings category will immediately appear in the list.

Fig.1.6 In this case only four images matched the search criteria

In Figure 1.6 I have expanded the Focal Length category by left-clicking it, and then I left-clicked the 260mm entry to select it. The four pictures in the folder that were taken at this focal length are shown in the main pane. You are not restricted to choosing one subcategory. Left-click a subcategory to select it, and left-click it again in order to deselect it. Selecting (say) the 50mm, 100mm and 210mm categories would result in any pictures in any one of those categories being selected.

Things work differently if you choose filters from more than one main category. For example, selecting the three focal lengths as before, but then choosing Portrait from the Orientation category would filter all images except those taken at one of the three selected focal lengths, and having portrait orientation. In other words, by using more than one filter category you can reduce the number of matches, and filter all or practically all the images that are not of interest.

Metadata

The Metadata panel shows information about the currently selected image. This data is stored within the image file by the camera at the time the photograph is taken. Note that with scanned images all or most of this data will not be available. Some of this data will probably not be available when taking photographs with a camera that is fitted with an

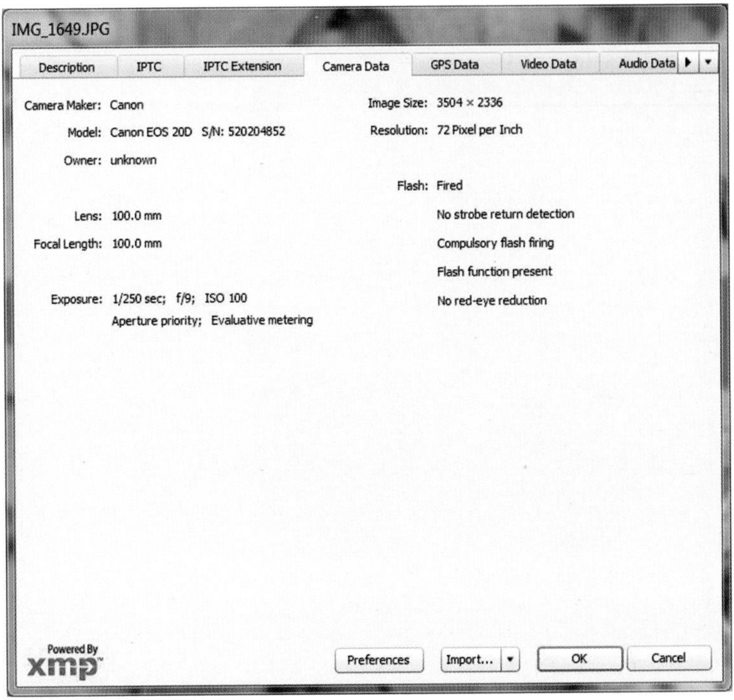

Fig.1.7 Using the File Info option to display the metadata

old lens that does not include any electronics to "talk" to the camera. An alternative way of showing the metadata for a file is to right-click its thumbnail and then select File Info from the pop-up menu. The metadata will be displayed in a new window (Figure 1.7).

Keywords

Keywords are used to categorise photographs so that you can search and sort your images according to these categories. There are some default categories and subcategories already present in the Keywords panel. A new category can be added via the "+" button at the bottom of the panel, or by right-clicking the blank area at the bottom of the panel and selecting New Keyword from the pop-up menu. Either way it is then just a matter of typing the keyword into the textbox that appears and then pressing the Return key.

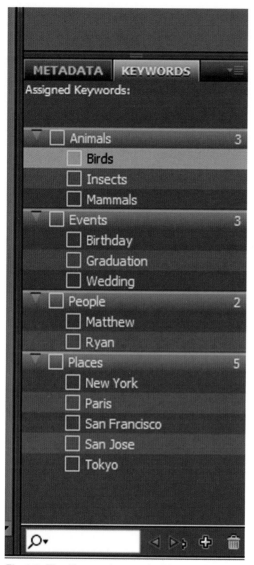

Fig.1.8 The Keywords panel with an added category

A subcategory can be added by selecting the appropriate keyword and then operating the button at the bottom of the panel that is immediately to the left of the "+" button. Alternatively, right-click the appropriate keyword and select New Sub Keyword from the pop-up menu. Again, it is then just a matter of typing the new word into the textbox that appears and then pressing the Return key. A keyword or sub keyword can be removed by right-clicking its entry and selecting Delete from the pop-up menu. Some of the default keywords are likely to be inappropriate and are best removed. In Figure 1.8 I have added an Animals keyword plus three sub keywords.

In order to associate a keyword or sub keyword with an image it is just a matter of selecting the image and then adding a tick to the

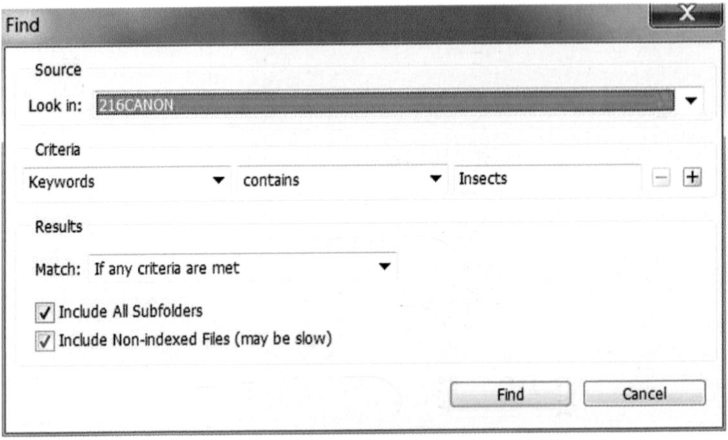

Fig.1.9 There are some options available from the Find window

appropriate checkbox or checkboxes in the Keywords panel. The normal multiple section methods can be used here. To display only the images associated with a certain keyword or sub keyword, right click the appropriate one in the Keyword panel and choose Find from the pop-up menu. A new window will appear (Figure 1.9), and it is just a matter of operating the Find button in order to display the matching images in the currently selected folder. There are various options available in the new window, such as selecting a different folder, and choosing whether or not to include any subfolders in the search.

Stacks

Thumbnail images can be stacked on top of each other in the main panel to conserve space (Figure 1.10). This is mainly done where there are a number of very similar images. In order to produce a stack it is just a matter of using the normal methods of multiple selection to choose the images, right clicking one of them, selecting Stack from the pop-up menu, and then choosing Group as Stack from the submenu.

Left clicking the button at the top left-hand corner of a stack expands it or restacks it again, as appropriate. Operating the arrow button automatically scrolls through all the stacked images, or you can scroll though them manually using the slider control. A stack can be undone by right clicking it and choosing Stack-Ungroup from Stack. The same method is used to remove an individual photo from its stack, but the

Fig.1.10 Images can be stacked

stack is first expanded, and then the individual image is selected.

In order to open an image in Photoshop it is just a matter of double-clicking its thumbnail. Alternatively, one or more images can be selected, one of them can be right-clicked, and then the Open option can be selected from the pop-up menu. Note that RAW images will be opened in the Camera RAW add-on and not in Photoshop.

Mini Bridge

Launching the Mini Bridge facility from within Photoshop results in the reduced version of Adobe Bridge appearing at the bottom of the main display area (Figure 1.11). This is really just a built-in file browser that has some limited filter ability. It can still be useful for finding images and loading them into Photoshop, but for most purposes it is better to use the full version of the program. The left-hand panel is used to select the required folder in standard Windows fashion, and the slider at the bottom of the screen is used to scroll through the images in the selected folder. An image can be opened in Photoshop by dragging its thumbnail into the main display area.

Fig.1.11 Mini Bridge is really just a built-in file browser

Basic editing

Home improvements

Although it has other features, I think it is fair to say that the vast majority of Photoshop users buy the program for its image editing facilities. It is not essential to do any editing of digital images, and there is no point in editing perfectly good images just for the sake of it. Getting over zealous with a photo-editing program can certainly result in what might be termed "a sow's ear from a silk purse". However, few images are perfect in their unprocessed form straight from the camera, and it is usually necessary to do at least a small amount of editing in order to get the best possible results from a digital camera. These days the average desktop PC is quite powerful and has a good quality colour display, making it well suited to photo editing. A good laptop or notebook computer should also work quite well in this application, although the relatively small screen size is less than ideal.

The camera manufacturers are now starting to include some image editing facilities in their digital cameras, but some photo editing software and a PC is needed in order to do the job really well. Adobe's Photoshop CS6 is the front runner at the professional end of the market. Being a piece of professional software it does not come cheap, but it offers a range of features and facilities that are proportionate to the price paid.

There are actually two versions of Photoshop, or three if you include the low cost Photoshop Elements program. The latter tends to be regarded as a stripped down version of the professional versions of Photoshop, which I suppose it is to some extent, but it is really a different program that has been tailored to suit a different market. It is aimed specifically at users of digital cameras who require a program that will enable them to optimise their photographs quickly and easily. It does actually have some advanced features, but it is primarily intended for those wishing to improve their images without delving too deeply into the intricacies of image editing. It lacks features such as macros, that enable a series of pre-recorded processes to be applied to an image simply by pressing one

Fig.2.1 Photoshop CS6 with the default screen layout and an image loaded

or two keys on the keyboard. In fairness to the developers of Photoshop Elements, it has to be pointed out that some of the features that originated in this "junior" program have found their way into the professional versions of Photoshop.

The two latest versions of the full Photoshop program are Photoshop CS6 and Photoshop CS6 Extended. The Extended version has extra 3D facilities, but it is otherwise the same as the standard version. The 3D extensions are not covered in this book, and the information contained herein therefore applies equally to either version of the program.

Hopeless cases

It is important to realise that although Photoshop is a very capable program, there are some images that are beyond redemption, and no computer program can work miracles. Remarkable improvements can often be made to images that have poor technical quality, but no photo editing program can bring out detail, colour, or other information that is simply not there in the original image. It is often possible to make artistic improvements to an image that is lacking in this respect, but again, it is unlikely that great improvements can be made to a picture that has no artistic merit. The idea is not to take awful pictures and then make them great using a battery of photo editing techniques. You should aim to get the best possible pictures, both artistically and technically, and then, where necessary, make them even better with Photoshop.

Basics

The Photoshop editing screen has a layout that is in most respects fairly standard for a modern Windows program, with a conventional menu bar at the top and a toolbar down the left-hand side of the screen. The large area to the right of the toolbar is used to display the picture that is being edited. To be more precise, it is used to display the picture or pictures that are being edited, because it is possible to have two or more photographs loaded at once. However, bear in mind that having several large images loaded into Photoshop can use large amounts of the computer's memory, and could result in the program slowing down very substantially.

The entire editing screen is known in Photoshop terminology as the "workspace", and although it looks something like Figure 2.1 by default, it can be customised to suit individual requirements. Existing elements of the layout can be switched off or moved, and new ones can be switched on. As you learn to use Photoshop it is virtually certain that changes to the workspace will be introduced, and you may well alter the workspace quite frequently as you customise it to suit different projects.

All the usual features are available via the menu bar, which has some standard Windows menu headings. It provides access to the usual facilities under the File menu, including Open, Save, and Print options. There is also a New option, which generates a blank picture area of the required size. It is possible to use the Photoshop as a paint program to create your own onscreen masterpieces, starting with a blank page, but as implied by the Photoshop name, it is not primarily aimed at this sort of thing. There are options to use the Bridge and Mini Bridge facilities, which were covered in Chapter 1.

Undo/Redo

The usual Windows Undo and Redo buttons do not seem to be included in Photoshop, but Undo and Redo options are still available in the Edit menu. As is now the case with many Windows programs, these are of the multi-level variety. In other words, if you do four or five pieces of editing and then change your mind, it is just a matter of using the Undo button four of five times in order to remove the unwanted changes. If you should then change your mind again, using the Redo button four or five times will reintroduce the changes.

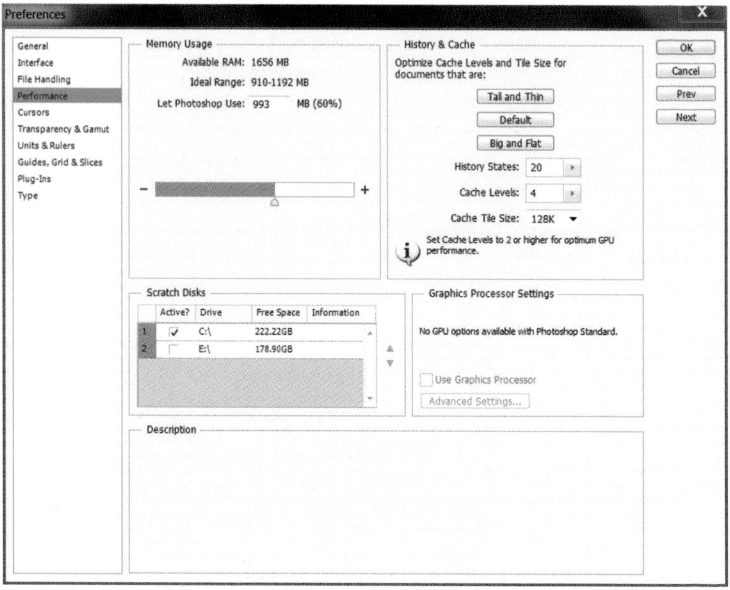

Fig.2.2 The Performance section of the Preferences window

Fig.2.3 Several stages of processing have been applied to this image

This is important, because it gives users the freedom to make changes, happy in the knowledge that they can be easily undone if they simply do not like the changes, or if it all goes disastrously wrong. There is a limit to the number of steps that can be undone and redone, and the default limit is 20 steps. The reason for having a limit is that storing details of each step uses the computer's resources, and in particular it can grab large amounts of the computer's memory.

It is possible to alter the maximum number of steps that can be undone by selecting Preferences from the Edit menu, and then choosing Performance from the submenu that appears. In the Preferences window (Figure 2.2) the History States can be set in the range 2 to 1000, but remember that using a high number could hog the computer's resources and result in things operating at greatly reduced speed once a large amount of editing has been undertaken. It could be beneficial to set a lower figure if you are using a computer that is equipped with a relatively small amount of memory.

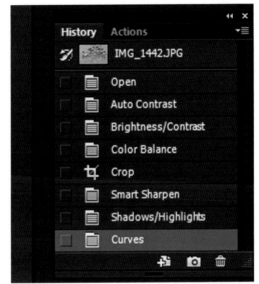

Fig.2.4 The History panel

History

There is a more sophisticated version of the Undo and Redo facilities in the form of the History panel. This is something that all Photoshop users need to be familiar with at an early stage. If it is not already displayed in the panels down the right-hand side of the screen, the History panel can be activated by selecting History from the Window menu. Like the other

Fig.2.5 The image has been taken right back to its initial state

Windows, it can be toggled on and off by selecting its entry in the Window menu. However, the History panel is so useful that it is probably best to switch it on and leave it that way.

The History panel makes it possible to freely experiment with images, happy in the knowledge that it is possible to go back a number of stages at the click of a mouse if you change your mind. Figure 2.3 shows the screen with an image that has undergone several stages of processing, and an enlarged version of the History panel is shown in Figure 2.4. In Figure 2.3 the History panel can be seen to the right of the image, and it lists the various changes that have been made to the image. In this case the number of changes made is less than 20, so it shows all the editing right back to when the image was opened. There is a brief description of each operation, such as Rotate Canvas or Sharpen, making it easy to go back to the required stage in the processing. Simply left-click on the appropriate entry in the History panel in order to go back to that stage of the processing. In Figure 2.5 the image has been taken right back to its initial state. It is possible to jump backward and forward as much as you like to any desired states in the list. In addition to undoing obvious errors, by jumping backward and forward between various stages of the editing it is easy to judge whether the "improvements" really have made the image better, or in reality have made no worthwhile difference.

The three buttons at the bottom of the History panel provide some useful features. Working from left to right, the first of them creates a new document using the current state as the starting point. You can therefore jump back to an earlier state and try again from there, leaving the original version fully intact. Bear in mind that going back to an earlier stage and continuing to edit from there effectively deletes the changes that were undone. With them gone from the History panel they are no longer available.

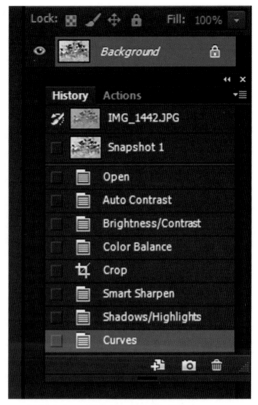

Fig.2.6 A snapshot has been added

The next button creates a new snapshot of the image at its current state. This snapshot appears near the top of the list of changes (Figure 2.6), and can be selected just like any of the other entries in the list. This can provide a "get out clause" if you go back to an earlier stage, start editing from there, and then decide you preferred your previous effort. Take a snapshot before going back and redoing the editing. If you change your mind it is just a matter of clicking the snapshot in order to revert to the previous editing, and there is no need to save a new version of the image to disc.

The snapshot facility is also useful because, as pointed out previously, Photoshop has a default limit of 20 changes in the History panel. Therefore, after a while, each new change results in an earlier one being deleted from the beginning of the list. This is done in order to prevent the History panel from using too much memory. Using the snapshot facility it is possible to jump back to strategic points in the development of the image, even if those points no longer appear in the list of changes.

It is possible to delete the selected state, and all subsequent ones, by operating the third button. You will be asked to confirm that you wish to make the deletions, so there is a chance to change your mind before obliterating a series of changes. This change is also reversible via the Undo facility if you should change your mind.

It is important to realise that the History panel has one or two limitations. As already pointed out, it only stores the last 20 changes, so there is a limit to how much you can undo. Even things like selecting an area using the Marquee tool, or deselecting it, count as changes. A few things, such as zooming and panning around the image, do not count as changes and cannot be reversed using the History panel. With any slightly involved editing the 20 changes will soon be used up. As pointed out previously, it is possible to increase the number of changes recorded, but this is likely to use up large amounts of the computer's resources and slow things down.

Another limitation to keep in mind is that the History panel is not saved with images. Consequently, it is not possible to undo changes that were made in a previous session working on that image. If you might need to rework images from earlier stages, make sure that you save separate copies of the image at each of those stages.

Menus

Some of the other menus are the type of thing found in many Windows programs, such as Edit, Help, and View. The others mainly provide access to editing features that are applied to the entire picture, or to a previously selected portion of the picture. The toolbar down the left-hand side of the screen also provides various editing facilities, but these are more selective in nature. For example, there are tools for selecting an area or several areas of the picture that can then be processed in some way, or for painting onto the picture in various ways.

There are various zoom options available under the View menu, but there is also a magnifier tool available in the toolbar, which is often the best choice when zooming in to examine part of the picture in detail. Not surprisingly, the magnifier tool is the one that has a picture of a magnifying glass as its icon (the fifth button from the bottom in the figure on page (viii)). As usual with toolbars, some hint text will appear if you place the pointer over an icon, and this tells you the function of the tool. In order to use the magnifier tool it is just a matter of using the mouse to drag a rectangle that covers the area of interest. That area will then fill the display area, which is the large blank section of the screen to the right of the toolbar.

Perhaps the most important of the zoom options in the View menu is the one called Actual Pixels. This zooms in on the image to an extent that results in each pixel of the image being matched to a single pixel of the displayed image. The point of using this feature is that it does not involve any of the compromises that usually occur when scaling an image up or down in size. You see a true representation of the image that is as accurate as your computer's display system can manage. When you need to assess the technical quality of an image, and particularly when judging its sharpness, the Actual Pixels view is all-important.

The problem with the Actual Pixels view, or any zooming in on the image, is that it is unlikely to fit into the area of the screen reserved for the picture. With something like a low resolution image for use on the Internet it is possible that it will fit into the display area for the picture, but the image from any reasonably modern digital camera is likely to be far too large. The number of pixels in the display area depends on the video generator and monitor you use, but it is unlikely to be more than about one or two million pixels.

Even the digital cameras of about ten years ago produced larger images than that, and today's digital wonder cameras usually have pixel counts in the 10 to 20 million range, and some exceed the 20 million mark. You can still view the full image, and choosing the Fit On Screen option from the View menu will result in the current image being displayed in its entirety and as large as possible in the available space.

Photoshop has a real-time pan feature that makes it easy to explore a zoomed image. This is accessed via the Hand tool in the toolbar, which you will probably not be surprised to learn is the one that has a hand icon on its button. This is the one above the zoom button in the figure on page (viii). There is a useful keyboard shortcut to this tool, which is to hold down the spacebar. The Hand tool will remain active for as long as the spacebar is pressed. The real-time panning feature operates in a manner that is a bit like having the full image behind a small window that enables only part of the image to be seen at any one time. The display area is the window, and the Hand tool enables the image to be dragged so that the desired section can be viewed. Of course, conventional horizontal and vertical scrollbars are available as well.

Fig.2.7 The panels can be moved to any position on the screen

Panels

Adobe software tends to make extensive use of floating panels, and Photoshop is certainly not an exception to this. The panels in use are normally positioned down the right-hand side of the screen, but as the "floating" name suggests, they can be dragged via the bar at the top and positioned anywhere on the screen (Figure 2.7). However, it is normally best just to settle for having them down the right-hand section of the screen. Numerous panels are available, making it necessary to only have a panel switched on if you are actually using it, or are likely to need it in the immediate future. As we have already seen with the History panel, the Window menu is used to toggle panels on and off.

The panels can be extremely useful when using Photoshop, but even when using a modest number of them they occupy a fair amount of space. If you start positioning them away from their allotted area of the screen you will soon have nowhere to display the image you are editing! Fortunately, Photoshop provides ways of using the panels section of the screen more effectively, so that a number of panels can be accommodated in their section of the screen. The bottom of each panel can be dragged so that the vertical size can be increased or reduced. Some panels have tabs at the top, and consist of two or three panels

Fig.2.8 The panels can be switched off

merged into one. Left-clicking a tab brings the corresponding panel to the fore. A panel can be dragged from a group so that it operates in isolation, and a solo panel can be dragged into a group.

Full screen

It is useful to remember that any panels on the screen can be toggled on and off using the Tab key. Things can be taken a stage further, and pressing the Shift and Tab keys simultaneously switches off everything except the menu bar, status bar and the display area (Figure 2.8). Press the Shift and Tab keys again to return the screen to normal. Switching off everything except the menu bar, status bar, and the display area gives something close to full screen operation with a huge area to display the image or images, but access to a large range of facilities is still possible via the menus. You can take things a stage further by selecting View-Screen Mode-Full Screen Mode from the menu system. This provides a true full screen mode where nothing but the image is displayed (Figure 2.9). Some control is still available via keyboard shortcuts, but the full screen facility is really included as a means of getting the best possible view of the complete picture for assessment purposes. It is not intended to be used when editing pictures. Press the Escape key to go from the full screen mode to the normal screen layout.

Fig.2.9 The full screen mode is precisely that, with nothing but the image being displayed

Instant results

Most programs that have some photo editing tools can provide a quick fix using some form of automatic editing facility. This will usually try to correct the exposure, maximise the contrast, and correct any colour cast. As one would probably expect, an automated system of this type does not always get everything absolutely right, and sometimes produces results that look ridiculous. The program providing the processing does not know whether the picture is of a group of people or a sunset, and the generalised rules it uses will not suit widely differing subject matter. On the other hand, there is no harm in trying automated processing. It provides a quick and easy solution when it works, and the processing can be instantly removed if the end result is useless.

Automatic correction works best when the subject matter is something fairly ordinary, and when the source images only need slight adjustment. It tends to be least effective with images that are unusual in some way, such as being predominantly one colour, and where a large amount of processing is required. With images that are well out of the ordinary, such as those of very low contrast scenes, the program will probably take the out of the ordinary aspect to be a fault and will try to correct it. A low contrast scene will be given a full range of tones and will probably look quite ridiculous. With images that need a lot of processing it will be necessary for the program to take a number of what are effectively guesses at the required processing, and it is quite likely to get it wrong at least once.

Auto Processing

Photoshop has three types of automatic processing, one of which could be regarded as a form of all-in-one fix. There are automatic adjustments available for tone, contrast and colour. The Auto Tone feature seems to be much the same as the Auto Levels facility of earlier versions of Photoshop. This is a type of all-in-one fix, but it is not as sophisticated as the similar features in some other photo editing programs. If you need a feature of this type you are actually better off with Photoshop Elements, which offers two types of all-in-one automatic processing.

Auto Contrast

The Auto Contrast facility is the one I would definitely rate as the most useful of the three automatic adjustments available in Photoshop. Contrast is an important aspect of photography, and it will therefore be considered in some detail here before progressing to the other types of automatic processing. The purpose of the Auto Contrast facility is to give "flat" images a full range of tones. However, it does so without burning out detail in the lighter parts of the picture, or blackening and losing detail in darker areas. Of course, if an inaccurate exposure or high contrast subject matter has already produced a loss of detail in the highlights or shadow areas, using the Auto Contrast facility will not restore this detail. It will give maximum contrast without making things any worse though.

There are various causes of a photograph not having a full range of tones, and in some instances it is simply that the subject matter is genuinely low in contrast. Often it is due to slight over or under exposure making the photograph generally too bright or too dark. It is quite common for digital cameras to err slightly in the direction of under exposure. This is not due to a fault, and it is the way they were designed to operate.

Slight overexposure results in detail being lost in the burned-out highlights, and no amount of processing will recover the missing detail. A small amount of under exposure will presumably lose a certain amount of detail in the darkest parts of the image, but in practice it is usually possible to "lift" a lot of detail from the dark areas of the picture. After a

Fig.2.10 This image is seriously under exposed

certain amount of processing it is quite likely that a slightly under exposed picture will look fine, but the same is not true of slightly over exposed pictures.

The photograph of Figure 2.10 is not too bad, but it has rather low contrast and is a bit dark. Sometimes there is an obvious cause of the problem, such as a large area of bright sky that has "fooled" the camera's automatic exposure system and left the foreground too dark. Here it just looks like a straightforward case of under exposure due to "pilot error". Using the automatic contrast system of Photoshop produced the image shown in Figure 2.11, which has boosted the contrast and lightened the picture a little. It might benefit from some further work, but it is a big improvement on the version of Figure 2.10, and is quite good as it is.

Fig.2.11 Using the Auto Contrast facility has made a big improvement

Mist opportunity

An automatic contrast facility will not always provide the desired effect, and it is not something that should be used with a photograph that quite correctly contains something less than a full range of tones. For example, the misty scene of Figure 2.12 has a rather limited range of tones, but this is only to be expected with a scene of this type. The image gives the impression that it was a very dull day with plenty of mist around, and this was the case. The picture is perhaps a little drab, but the lack of contrast is correct.

Boosting it to a full range using an automatic contrast system provided the result shown in Figure 2.13. This version is more dramatic, but it does not really have a great deal in common with the original scene.

Fig.2.12 This image lacks contrast, but accuately reflects the original scene

The mist in the middle distance and foreground has miraculously disappeared! Using high contrast on a low contrast scene will often give a more dramatic or prettier picture, but it will not be a true representation of the original scene, or anything approximating to it.

Of course, in some circumstances an artificial boost in contrast can be very desirable. If you refer back to Figure 2.5 there is a picture taken on a very misty day, and although it is faithful to the original scene, it does not really work that well pictorially. The processed version of Figure 2.3 has increased contrast and colour saturation, and is the one I think most people would rate as the better of the two pictures. Photographs taken using older lenses often lack contrast. In some cases they never did have good contrast by modern standards, but usually it is a result of the lens coatings deteriorating and (or) dirt of some sort in the lens. Provided the lens has good sharpness, a boost in contrast and a small increase in the colour saturation will usually produce good results from a lens that seems to have exceeded is "use by" date.

Over the top

An automatic contrast facility will sometimes provide an effect that is clearly "over the top", and into the realms of special effects. This will

Fig.2.13 Boosting the contrast has produced a prettier but less accurate picture

occur if a full range of tones is applied to a photograph that quite correctly contains a fairly limited range of tones. For example, the foggy scene of Figure 2.14 has a rather restricted range of tones, but this is only to be expected with a scene of this type. The image gives the impression that it was a very dull day with lots of thick fog around, and it was. The picture is definitely a little drab, but the lack of contrast is correct.

Boosting it to a full range using an automatic contrast system provided the result shown in Figure 2.15. Once again, this version is more dramatic, but it does not really have a great deal in common with the original scene. The fog in the middle distance and foreground, despite being quite dense in the middle distance, has miraculously disappeared! The image is more dramatic than the original, and might be considered to be a better picture in some ways, but it is even less faithful to the original scene than the two previous examples.

Brightness/Contrast

Where more subtle changes in brightness and (or) contrast are required it is necessary to resort to manual adjustment, and Photoshop has conventional brightness and contrast controls. These are available from the Image menu (Image-Adjustments- Brightness/Contrast). There are

Fig.2.14 This picture of a boat in the fog quite correctly has a low level of contrast

slider controls for adjusting the brightness and contrast (Figure 2.16), and it is really just a matter of using trial and error to find the settings that give the best result. The two settings interact in a way that often results in a great deal of going to and fro between the two controls before you finally end up with the desired result.

Fig.2.15 The effect of using Auto Contrast is completely "over the top"

In Figure 2.17 I have tweaked the brightness and contrast slightly in an attempt to add a little more contrast and tame the brightness. I have also adjusted the colour balance slightly. The changes are not that great, but it gives a finished result that is much closer to the way I remember the original scene. The boat stands out a little more from the background. The yellow colour of its hull was clearly visible when looking at the original scene, but was practically lost in the unedited image. The manual editing has made it a bit more noticeable.

Darkening

Figure 2.18 shows a shot of the two butterflies, but this has the opposite problem to the example of Figure 2.10. The camera was accidentally knocked from auto to manual exposure, and this has resulted in an over exposed image. Fortunately, the degree of over exposure is not very high, but it has resulted in the picture being generally too light. Also, some of the brightest areas are burned out to pure white. There is nothing that can be done about this second point, but the main areas that have become burned out are shiny parts of leaves that are reflecting the bright sky. There is no detail of importance in these areas, and they still give the right effect in that the leaves still look shiny.

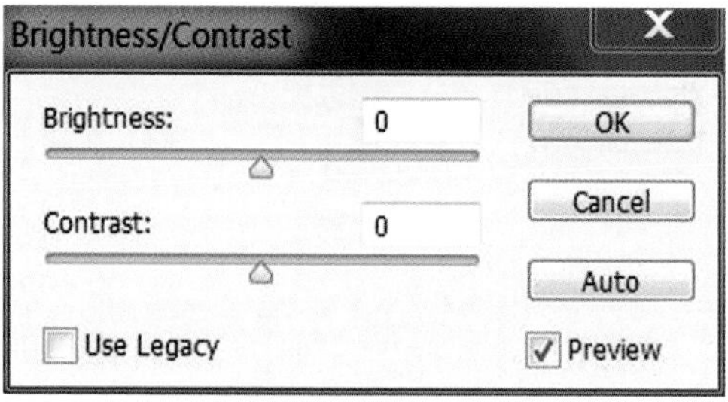

Fig.2.16 The Brightness/Contrast window

With an over exposed photograph of this type the Auto Contrast facility will generally darken the picture, hopefully revealing some extra details in the brighter parts of the picture as part of this process. In this example the change is not huge (Figure 2.19), but it has certainly made a great improvement to the image. However, some further processing would probably improve things further. One way of tackling the problem is to take the fully manual approach using brightness and contrast adjustments. However, using the Highlights control is usually quicker and easier, and mostly gives excellent results.

Highlights

The Highlights control is accessed via the Image menu (Image-Adjustments – Shadows/Highlights). There are actually two controls on

Fig.2.17 The manually adjusted version of the photograph

the small control panel that this produces (Figure 2.20), and the Shadows
control will be advanced to fifty percent by default. In the current context
this will almost certainly make matters much worse rather than better, so
it should be set at zero. The Highlights control is advanced to give the

Fig.2.18 This photograph is a little over exposed

desired result. In Figure 2.21 I have advanced it enough to bring out a little more detail in some of the lighter areas, and this slightly darker version of the picture is a little easier on the eye when viewed on a large computer monitor.

Exposure

The Exposure control is accessed via the Adjustments submenu (Image-Adjustments-Exposure). It can be used to compensate for underexposure (too dark) or overexposure (too bright), but there will almost certainly be some loss of detail if there is anything more than a slight exposure error. Large exposure errors will cause clipping and a loss of highlight detail in overexposed images, and shadow detail in under exposed types. The calibration of the Exposure control is in stops, but it is really a matter of adjusting it "by eye" for the best result. It will probably be impossible to obtain worthwhile results if more than about two stops of compensation are needed. In the case of over exposure, even an error of two stops could render the image irretrievable.

Fig.2.19 Using Auto Contrast has slightly darkened the image

The exposure window also has two additional controls, which are the Offset and Gamma types. The Offset control alters the brightness, but it affects the darkest areas far more than the mid tones and highlights. In other words, it can be used to lighten or darken shadows, but any more than very slight adjustment of this control is likely to be a mistake. The Gamma control mainly affects the mid tones, and can therefore be used to lighten or darken the image without introducing clipping. Again, it needs to be used sparingly. Although the Exposure window is the obvious place to go when editing

Shadows/Highlights		
Shadows		**OK**
Amount: 35 %		**Cancel**
		Load...
Highlights		**Save...**
Amount: 0 %		✓ Preview
☐ Show More Options		

Fig.2.20 The Shadows/Highlights window

Fig.2.21 The photograph has been darkened using the Highlights control

photographs that are incorrectly exposed, better results can often be achieved using facilities such as Curves and Levels.

Colour saturation

When editing photographs, and particularly when making adjustments to the brightness and contrast, there can be problems with the colour saturation. Looking at things as simply as possible, the colour saturation is the strength of the colours. Weak colours that have low saturation are effectively diluted with grey, giving them a rather washed out appearance. Strong colours have high purity and are very lively looking. When making adjustment to the brightness and (or) contrast of an image you will often find that there is an apparent reduction in the general degree of colour saturation. Less commonly, the colours might seem to become excessively strong.

Photoshop has a colour saturation control that is available via the Image menu (Image-Adjustments–Hue/Saturation). There are actually three

Fig.2.22 Using zero saturation produces a black and white image

slider controls in the pop-up Hue/Saturation panel (near the bottom right corner of the screen in Figure 2.22), but for the moment we will only consider the Saturation control, which is the middle one. It is a bit like a volume control for colour, and taking it fully to the left removes the colour altogether and gives a monochrome image, as in Figure 2.22. Taking the saturation control further to the right produces stronger colours, but it is best not to get carried away and produce images that have so-called "Mickey Mouse" colours. Taking things still further can sometimes give very odd looking results.

In Figure 2.23 I have advanced the Saturation control slightly in order to strengthen the colours, which it has done. The saturation control operates in a very simple manner, and the problem with adding saturation to the weaker colours is that it also boosts those that are already quite strong. This has certainly occurred in this example. Using the saturation control is often a matter of selecting a good compromise between strengthening the weaker colours on the one hand, and avoiding excessive boosting of the medium and stronger colours on the other hand.

The slider beneath the Saturation control is the Lightness control, which despite its name can be used to lighten or darken an image. It is useful to have the Saturation and Lightness controls on the same control panel since you can make changes to the brightness and then immediately

Fig.2.23 Here the colour saturation has been increased

make any necessary adjustment to the saturation level. With a certain amount of going to and fro from one control to the other it should be possible to quickly obtain the desired result. In theory, lightening an image will often require the saturation to be increased slightly, and reducing the brightness will usually require a small decrease. Things do not necessarily work this way in every instance though, and it obviously applies only when the colour saturation level is about right to start with.

Vibrance

Photo editing software often has a vibrance control, which is a more sophisticated version of the saturation type. Rather than treating all areas of colour equally, a vibrance control has more effect with weaker colours than those of medium saturation, and it has little or no effect with areas where the colour saturation is high. This makes it possible to boost weak colours without sending the stronger areas of colour "over the top". A vibrance control is usually designed to have little effect with skin tones. This makes it possible to boost or reduce the colour saturation of

Fig.2.24 The colours in this image are slightly on the weak side

other elements in a picture without making the people look either very ill
or extremely embarrassed! Photoshop has an excellent vibrance control
that can be accessed by way of the Image menu (Image-Adjustments-
Vibrance).

Fig.2.25 Adding vibrance has strengthened the colours

The photograph of Figure 2.24 has strong colour in the red hull of the boat, but there are mainly weak colours elsewhere. The early morning sun shining on the boat in the background should be much more yellow in colour. The green seaweed in the bottom right-hand corner is not all

*Fig.2.26 Increased saturation has improved most of the picture, but
the red hull of the boat is over-saturated*

that green, and that part of the picture looks to be almost in monochrome.
In Figure 2.25 the vibrance level has been set at maximum, giving an
improvement in the colours without over-saturating the red in the boat's
hull. In fact there is very little change in this part of the photograph.

Fig.2.27 Using minimum saturation still leaves some colour

The same is not true of the version in Figure 2.26 where increased colour saturation has been used in place of increased vibrance. This has perhaps done a slightly better job in many parts of the image, but the hull of the boat in the foreground looks far from natural. In addition to the red of the hull being far too strong in colour, detail has been lost in areas where the colour has reached maximum saturation. In Figure 2.27 the vibrance control has been set at minimum. Notice how most of the colour has been removed, but the picture has not been converted into a black and white type. The strong reds in the hull of the boat have been changed very little, giving an interesting effect for those who like that type of thing.

It is not necessarily a matter of adjusting the vibrance setting or the saturation level in order to optimise results. Sometimes using a combination of these two adjustments will give the best results. Both controls are available from the Vibrance control window, making it easy to use them together. It should be noted that vibrance can only be adjusted in the RGB colour mode, and that it is not available in the CMYK colour mode.

Colour balance

Often problems with the colours in an image are not due to an error in the saturation levels, but are instead due to a more fundamental problem. Severe problems with colour are more likely to be due to a colour cast. Digital cameras have various white balance options, but most users just settle for the automatic option. These are generally quite good at assessing the prevailing light and setting a suitable white balance so that the pictures displayed on the screen of your monitor reflect the way things looked when the picture was taken.

On the face of it, there is no need for any adjustments to the colours in a photograph, and everything should be fine if the camera simply records things the way they were. In practice it is not as simple as that. Tungsten lighting has a strong red content when compared to typical daylight, and fluorescent lighting is usually quite green in colour. You tend not to notice this when you are in a room that is lit by either of these light sources, because your eyes and brain adjust to the colour of the lighting and accept it as normal.

If you take a photograph using either of these types of artificial light they will probably not look right to most people unless some adjustment is made to the colours. The colours may well be true to the originals, but on the photograph they are being viewed out of context by people who have not adjusted their perception to match the conditions when the photograph was taken. A picture taken under tungsten lighting will look too orange/red, and one taken under some form of fluorescent lighting will tend to look too green, probably with some rather odd looking colours being produced.

*Fig.2.28 Automatic colour correction has produced a rather "cold"
result in this example*

A camera's automatic white balance system tries to produce natural colours that will look right when you view the photograph on the screen of a computer or in the form of a print. This feature has to be regarded as something of a mixed blessing. In the right context it will have the desired effect, but it will sometimes kill the mood of an image. Natural light can be quite blue on a dull day or when there is a blue sky but the sun is obscured by cloud. At sunrise and sunset it can be very red in colour due to the filtering effect of dust particles in the atmosphere. At other times it can be anywhere between these two extremes. These different colours of light give a scene atmosphere, and the automatic white balance feature of a camera can sometimes alter the colour balance and totally change the mood of an image. The reds and oranges of a sunset can be altered to give a picture that has the sun near the horizon, but otherwise looks as if it was taken at midday!

Digital cameras usually have alternatives to an automatic white balance control. One of these should be a natural setting, where the white balance is left untouched. When you are trying to capture the mood of a scene this is usually a better option that an automatic white balance control,

Fig.2.29 This photograph has a slight blue/green tinge

and it can avoid having to correct the erroneous corrections made by an automatic white balance system. Use the automatic system when the lighting is in some way unusual and is likely to need some correction in order to obtain natural looking results.

Auto Color

As pointed out previously, automatic colour adjustment is one of the three types of automated processing available from Photoshop. However, like the automatic white balance feature of a camera, it will not always provide the desired result. There is no harm in trying this feature, since it can be undone using the History panel or the Undo facility. Photoshop does not know whether the image is a seascape or a bunch of flowers, a spectacular sunset or a predominantly green cricket pitch at midday, so an automatic colour balance facility inevitably involves some technical guesswork. Sometimes it will be right or quite close, but often the results will be a long way out.

In order to try out this feature it is just a matter of going to the Image menu and selecting the Auto Color option. This feature is fully automatic,

Fig.2.30 The Auto Color facility has worked better in this example

and it is not possible to make any manual adjustments to the way it operates. Applying automatic colour correction to the edited picture of the two butterflies produced the result shown in Figure 2.28. The photograph was taken on a summer's day in the late afternoon, which is why the original image, Figure 2.18, is rather yellow in colour. This helps to give the picture a summery feel, and is not something that needs to be corrected. The yellow cast of the original image is perhaps a little strong, but this is better than the version of Figure 2.28 where the colours are rather "cold", and the bluish colour balance has lost the summery feel of the original. It has also produced some rather "washed out" looking colours. In general, automatic colour correction facilities tend to produce a rather "cold" colour balance.

The Auto Color facility has worked better in Figure 2.29 where the image has a slight blue/green tinge. Automatically correcting the colours has produced the better result of Figure 2.30. The difference is not huge, but it has tamed the slightly unnatural colours in the sea and the sky. Of the two images, the version of Figure 2.30 certainly looks more like the original scene.

Fig.2.31 This image has low contrast and a slight yellow cast

Auto Tone

If you experiment with the Auto Tone facility it might seem to be much the same as the Auto Contrast type. It does actually optimise the contrast of an image, but it does so by processing the three colour channels separately. The colour picture on a monitor is produced by mixing the three primary colours (red, green, and blue) in various strengths, and this enables millions of different colours to be produced. The Auto Tone facility adjusts each of the primary colours so that it has the full range of tones from so dark that it is black through to so light that it is white. Because the three primary colours are adjusted separately, and will in most cases be changed in different ways, there will be some degree of colour shift in addition to a boost in contrast. This shift might correct an unwanted colour cast, or it could introduce one!

The butterfly photograph of Figure 2.31 is rather low in contrast and has a yellowish colour cast. I am not sure why this has happened, because the dozen or so other photographs I took of the butterfly on the same flower did not have this problem to anything like the same degree. Anyway, applying Auto Contrast to the image did not make much difference (Figure 2.32). Although the image looks rather "flat", I presume that the black and white parts of the butterfly give high contrast in small parts of the picture. These small areas of high contrast prevent the Auto

Fig.2.32 Using the Auto Contrast facility has made little difference

*Fig.2.33 Additionally using the Auto Color facility has not had the
desired effect. The yellow cast has been replaced by a
stronger red/magenta one*

Fig.2.34 Using the Auto Tone facility has worked quite well

Contrast facility from making anything more than a minor adjustment. In Figure 2.33 the Auto Color facility has been added to the Auto Contrast adjustment made previously. This has not really had the desired effect, with a yellow cast being replaced by an even worse red/magenta one.

In Figure 2.34 the original image has been processed using the Auto Tone facility. This has worked quite well with the image appearing to have much better contrast. The colours are also much improved, with the butterfly having lost its greenish tinge. If anything it is perhaps a little too blue, but the image works quite well that way, and any manual "fine tuning" of the colour would probably be pointless.

Using Auto Tone on an image will often give something close to the desired effect, or will have very little effect, but it can sometimes produce completely hopeless results. The picture of the ship in Figure 2.35 is not too bad in its unedited form, but an increase in contrast and perhaps some slight adjustment of the colour balance might improve matters. Using the Auto Tone facility (Figure 2.36) has not really had the desired effect. The contrast has improved, but the sea and the bluish haze in the background have been made a very unrealistic and over-saturated blue/ purple colour. In this instance using the Auto Contrast feature instead (Figure 2.37) has produced a more subtle but much better change to the picture.

Fig.2.35 The unprocessed photograph of a ship

Fig.2.36 Using the Auto Tone facility has made the image far too blue

Fig.2.37 Applying Auto Contrast has given a better result in this case

Halfway house

Sometime using Auto Tone produces the correct changes, but does not go far enough. The picture in Figure 2.38 is of an ant on a thistle, but it is so under exposed that you will probably have to study it quite closely in order to see the ant. The flashgun failed to fire and the picture was exposed using only natural light. Using Auto Tone on the image has produced a big improvement (Figure 2.39), but there is still a bluish cast, and it is still rather dark. One option in cases such as these is to simply abandon the automatic approach completely by undoing the Auto Tone command and using manual editing.

However if an automatic process gets you closer to the desired result it is probably best to leave the automatic changes in place and use them as a "halfway house". Manual editing from the improved version of the picture is likely to be much quicker and easier than going back to the original image and starting from scratch. In Figure 2.40 I have made some simple manual adjustments to the version of Figure 2.39, such as reducing the amount of blue and increasing the colour saturation. This has rendered the ant more visible and has produced colours that are closer to those of the original scene.

Fig.2.38 This photograph is massively under exposed

Fig.2.39 Using the Auto Tone facility has greatly improved the image, but there is still room for improvement

Fig.2.40 Some manual adjustments have made further improvements

Auto Levels/Curves

In addition to the three automatic adjustments covered previously, there are two more that can be obtained via the Levels (Image-Adjustments-Levels) and Curves (Image-Adjustments-Curves) features. These are both more advanced versions of conventional brightness and contrast controls. The ways in which they are used to make manual adjustments is covered later in this book and it will not be considered here.

There is an Auto button available from

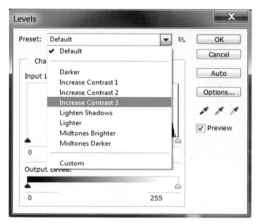

Fig.2.41 Preset options in the Levels window

Fig.2.42 The effect of the Contrast 3 option is relatively subtle

the Levels window, but in the current context it is the Preset menu of this window (Figure 2.41) that is perhaps of most interest. This offers preset adjustments for such things as lightening and darkening an image, plus three different contrast adjustments. Figure 2.42 shows the image of

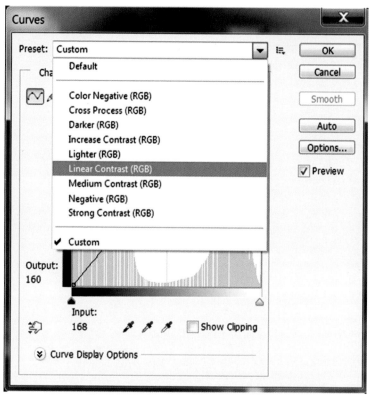

Fig.2.43 The Curves window also has some preset adjustments

Figure 2.14 with the Contrast 3 option applied. Its effect is much more subtle than the one obtained using Auto Contrast (Figure 2.15). There are more features available from the Levels window, including a Custom option in the Presets menu that enables the user to design their own preset adjustment, and the Options button provides various algorithms that can be used as the basis of adjustments.

The Curves feature is one of the most powerful available from Photoshop, and it gives tremendous control over the brightness and contrast of an image. You will certainly not get the most from this feature via its preset automation, but this aspect of it can be quite useful nevertheless. Like the Levels window, the Curves one has some preset adjustments available from a drop-down menu (Figure 2.43).

Fig.2.44 A picture of a poppy with the Negative option applied

The Cross Processing and Negative options are into the realms of special effects. Figure 2.44 shows a picture of a red poppy that has been processed using the Negative option. The Negative option seems to have exactly the same effect as the Invert command (Image-Adjustments-Invert). It could be useful for converting scanned colour negatives into positive images, but it will not correct the built-in colour cast and low contrast of most negative films. This seems to be the purpose of the Color Negative option.

Equalize

The Equalize command (Image-Adjustments-Equalize) provides another form of automatic adjustment. Its basic function is to make the darkest pixel in an image black, and the lightest white, with everything in between being changed accordingly. It is perhaps not one of the more highly regarded features of Photoshop, and like any automated adjustment, it will sometimes produce useless results.

In Figure 2.45 the dark image of Figure 2.10 has been processed using the Equalize command. It is a case of "out of the frying pan and into the fire", with the under exposure being replaced with over exposure. The

Fig.2.45 In this example the Equalize facility has overdone things

Equalize command has worked better in Figure 2.46, where it has been used on the image of Figure 2.38. The result is a bit on the light side and the colours are weak, but a lot of detail has been recovered from what was technically a very poor original image. A boost in colour saturation and a minor adjustment using the Highlight control was sufficient to give an acceptable image (Figure 2.47).

Shadows control

The Highlights control is used to darken the brightest parts of an image and, with luck, recover a certain amount of detail from the highlights. It was featured previously in this chapter. The Highlight control is accompanied by the Shadows control, and they are accessed via the Image menu (Image-Adjustments-Shadows/Highlights). I think it is fair

Fig.2.46 The Equalize facility has worked better in this example

Fig.2.47 Some manual adjustments to the image of Fig.2.46 has given
a further improvement

Fig.2.48 The problem here is caused by the main subject being backlit, effectively making it under exposed

to say that the Shadows control is the more useful of the two, and the main reason for this is that many digital cameras tend to err on the side of under exposure. This is done deliberately by the designers, and the reason is that it is often possible to recover detail from slightly under exposed areas of an image.

The same is not true of highlights that have been slightly over exposed and have "burned out" to pure white. Using the Highlights control or something of the same ilk to darken the brightest parts of a picture will produce an end result that looks much better than the original, but in most cases there will be little or no extra detail in evidence. The Shadows control cannot bring out details from areas of a picture that are totally black, but in practice it is often possible to "lift" a lot of detail from areas that seemed to be virtually black and featureless.

The picture of a coot shown in Figure 2.48 is correctly exposed, but has slight problems due to the plumage of the bird being black, and the shot being more or less backlit. The sun is actually quite high in the sky because the photograph was taken at around midday at the height of summer, but it has still left much of the coot's body in shadow. In Figure 2.49 I have used the Shadow control to lighten the darkest areas of the picture. This has helped to give a bit more shape to the body of the

Fig.2.49 Using the Shadows control has given a slight improvement

*Fig.2.50 The high contrast of this scene has produced some very dark
shadow areas that show very little detail*

Fig.2.51 Using the Shadows control has brought out more detail, but this version is less moody than the original

coot, but much of its head is so dark and in shadow that it is never going to be anything other than a silhouette.

On the face of it, the image of Figure 2.50 is the type of thing where the Shadow control can be used to lighten the dark areas of the picture to bring out more detail and produce a big improvement. The adjusted version of Figure 2.51 certainly has more detail than the original, but it does not really work too well as a picture. The slightly "over the top" contrast of the original produces a good effect with the lighter parts in the sunlight standing out from the dark shadow areas. This captures the mood of the original scene far better than the processed version. Some further processing could be used to get back some of the lost atmosphere, but it would probably produce something quite close to the original version. With this type of photograph it might actually be better to use the Highlights control instead of the Shadows type (Figure 2.52). This will perhaps bring out a bit more colour and detail in the highlights, and make the lighter mid tones a bit darker so that the highlights stand out from them even better.

The photograph of Figure 2.53 works quite well as it stands, but the shape of the tyres has been lost slightly in the large areas of deep shadow. In Figure 2.54 I have used the Shadows control to lighten these dark

Fig.2.52 Using the Highlights control is in some ways better

Fig.2.53 This image has some very dark shadow areas

Fig.2.54 *Using the Shadows control has helped to lighten the shadows
and give more shape to the types*

Fig.2.55 *An increase in colour saturation can help to put back any
dynamism lost by using the Shadows control*

Fig.2.56 This photograph has a greenish tinge

areas, and have also used the Highlights control to get a bit more detail in the very bright areas along the tops of the tyres. I am not sure if I really prefer the edited version, but it does show the shape of the tyres better, and technically it is the better of the two.

Using the Shadows control to a significant extent often produces rather "flat" looking images with an apparent lack of contrast. This is simply due to some of the darker areas being lightened so that they are virtually mid-tones, but the mid-tones are lightened very little. Although the overall contrast of the picture remains unchanged, in many areas of the picture the local contrast is greatly reduced, producing a rather "flat" result. Some of the colours can also become a bit pale with a "washed-out" appearance. This effect is not very noticeable in Figure 2.54, but is very pronounced in Figure 2.51. An increase in the colour saturation, perhaps in conjunction with an adjustment to the vibrance, will often improve matters. In Figure 2.55 I have probably gone a bit too far, but it shows how increased colour saturation can help to put back any dynamism lost by using the Shadows control.

*Fig.2.57 Using the neutral grey eyedropper has replaced the green
tinge with a red one*

Eyedropper

The Levels function can be used in an automatic mode where the colour
balance as well as the brightness is adjusted. The automatic operation
is achieved with the aid of the Eyedropper tool. The basic idea is to
indicate a point on the image that should be black, white, or a mid-grey
colour. Photoshop then automatically adjusts the colour balance and
brightness of the image so that the selected spot is the right colour, and
this should remove the colour cast from the image.

This method is not totally reliable in practice, since it is dependent on
the user finding a spot on the image that should be pure black or white,
or a neutral grey at a mid-tone. Finding a suitable grey is quite difficult,
and there may not be a suitable colour on the image. The photograph of
Figure 2.56 has a greenish tinge, and the blue/green colouring in the
darker areas of snow should be closer to a pure blue. Using the neutral
grey eyedropper on likely looking parts of the picture was not very
successful, and tended to exchange a green cast for a red type (Figure
2.57).

Fig.2.58 This photograph has a mild blue colour cast

Most images have something very close to pure black or white, or what would be pure black or white if there was no colour cast, and using one of these is a more practical option. However, an area that looks as though it should be black or white may actually have slight coloration, and quite rightly have some coloration. This colour will be removed by the processing, and the whole image will be given the same treatment. The colour cast will not be accurately counteracted, and once again a new colour cast will be introduced. Another potential problem is that what appears to be black might actually be dark grey, and an apparently white area might be very pale grey. This can result in unacceptable lightening or darkening of the image. Of course, if things do not go perfectly the first time, the processing can be removed and another spot on the image can be used as the reference point. Sometimes this method works, but with some images there are no suitable reference colours.

Near the bottom right-hand corner of the Levels window, Figure 2.41, there are three eyedropper tools available, and from left to right these are used with black, mid-grey, and white levels. To apply colour correction the appropriate eyedropper button is selected and then a suitable point on the image is selected using the eyedropper tool. In my experience this method of colour correction usually works best using the black as the reference colour. Therefore, I use the black eyedropper tool first and

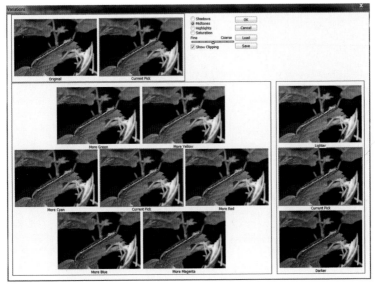

Fig.2.59 The Variations window

then the white one if the initial attempts are unsuccessful. With most images it is possible to find a good black level to use as the reference, and the colour cast is then instantly removed.

Even if the correction is not perfect, this method will usually get quite close to the correct colour balance, and some "fine tuning" can then be applied using another method. It is much easier than applying all the colour correction "by eye".

The channel menu enables the individual primary colours to be selected and processed separately. Presumably it would be possible to automatically adjust the balance of each channel using mid-tone primary colours as references, but these will not be present in most images. Adjusting the settings for each channel permits the colour balance to be adjusted manually, but this is not the only way of manually adjusting the colour balance.

Variations

Variations is an option in the Adjustments submenu (Image-Adjustments-Variations), and it also provides a relatively simple means of adjusting the colour balance. The photograph of Figure 2.58 has some lovely

Fig.2.60 The yellow level and brightness have been increased

strong blues in the body of the damselfly, which is not surprising as the whole image seems to have a bluish colour cast. The greens in the leaves for example, should be a mid or slightly yellowish green, but are actually a blue - green colour.

Selecting the Variations feature produces the pop-up window of Figure 2.59. The top section of the window shows the original image and the modified version, but these will be the same initially. The lower section of the window shows six variations that have extra red, green, blue, cyan, magenta, and yellow. It is possible but unlikely that one of these variations will be exactly what is required. In that event, it is just a matter of left clicking on the appropriate version, and the modified image will then adjust to match it. Operate the OK button to return to the image and make the changes take effect.

In most cases some adjustments will be required in order to get a really good colour balance. The basic colour casts are quite strong, but they can be weakened or made even stronger by adjusting the slider control near the top middle section of the window. Left clicking on one of the tinted images two or three times is another way of obtaining stronger effects. You are not limited to one type of correction, and can also left-click on different images to combine two tints.

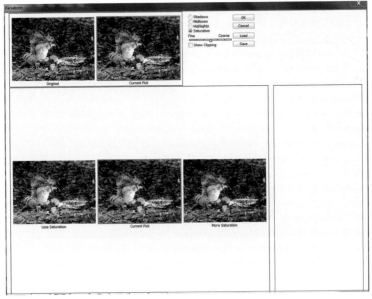

Fig.2.61 The degree of colour saturation can also be changed

Left clicking on the lighter and darker images in the bottom right-hand section of the window respectively lightens or darkens the modified image. Again, left clicking two or three times gives a stronger effect, and the slider control can be used to vary the amount of change per mouse click. With both the colour balance and the brightness you can either settle for something that is not totally adequate but is passable, or you can gradually "fine tune" the image until it is exactly as required.

It is just a matter of left clicking on the unmodified image if you would like to remove all the processing and start again from scratch. The OK button is operated when the desired effect is obtained, or the Cancel button is operated if you change your mind and wish to abandon the processing. In this example I settled for increasing the yellow level by a modest amount and slightly lightening the image, giving the result shown in Figure 2.60.

There are four radio buttons above the slider control, and three of these enable the mid-tones, shadows of highlights to be adjusted. The default is for the mid-tones to be adjusted, which is usually all you will need to do, but the other two options are there if you need them. There is also a

Fig.2.62 The rose picture with no adjustments made

Saturation option here, and the window changes to look like Figure 2.61 when this is selected. This operates in much the same way as before, but there are only two thumbnail images, and these give increased colour saturation (the right-hand one) or decreased saturation (the left-hand one). The slider control enables the amount of change to be varied. It is useful to have a colour saturation control available from within the colour variations feature, but it provides a rather clumsy method of control. For most purposes the ordinary colour saturation control is a more convenient way of handling things.

Hue control

The Hue control is available from the Adjustments submenu (Image-Adjustments-Hue/Saturation). The Saturation control was covered previously in this chapter and will not be considered any further here. The Hue control provides a means of altering the colour balance. It can produce subtle changes, massive changes, or anything in between.

I think it is fair to say that the Hue control is a bit confusing. If you try experimenting with various settings it will probably appear to be producing random colour changes. The two colour bars at the bottom of the window were not placed there to make it look pretty, and if you move the Hue control to the right the lower colour bar will shift to the left. The picture of

Fig.2.63 The colour balance has been shifted in the yellow direction

two roses shown in Figure 2.62 is used as the basis of this example, and in Figure 2.63 the Hue control has been moved to the right. This has duly resulted in the lower colour bar being shifted out of alignment to the

Fig.2.64 Moving the slider in the other direction gives more red

Fig.2.65 Extreme settings give a colour negative effect

left. In Figure 2.64 the hue control has been moved to the left, and the lower colour bar has moved to the right.

What the two colour bars are showing are the input and output colours. With the Hue control at a central setting the two bars are aligned and the input colour is always the same as the output colour. Move the control slightly to the left and yellow on the top bar (the input colour) is vertically aligned with orange on the lower bar (the output colour). There is a similar shift right across the spectrum. Move the Hue control slightly to the right and things are reversed, with orange being replaced with yellow, etc.

These small adjustments give what artists term warmer colours if the Hue control is moved to the left or colder colours if it is moved to the right. In other words, more red and more blue respectively. I find this is useful for adjusting skin tones. Skin tones that are too red giving a "lobster" effect can be corrected by moving the Hue control to the right. Slightly green and unnatural skin tones can usually be corrected by moving the Hue control fractionally to the left. More than slight changes produce massive colour shifts, and you are then into the realm of special effects (Figure 2.65). Moving the control fully left or right produces a colour negative, but not a negative in terms of brightness. In other words, the colours are reversed, but light areas remain light, and dark areas will still be dark.

Fig.2.66 In the original image the flower is a purple colour

So far it has been assumed that colour and brightness changes will be applied to the entire image, but the Hue control is often used with selected parts of an image. Using the selection tools of Photoshop is covered in

Fig.2.67 The Hue control has been used to change the colour of the flower

Fig.2.68 The flower has been changed to yellow using just the Hue control

the next chapter, and it will not be considered in detail here. In Figure 2.66 the Quick Selection tool has been used to select the flower head, but nothing else. In Figure 2.67 the Hue control has been adjusted to the right, which has resulted in the flower head changing from purple to red. The rest of the image remains unchanged, and the foliage is still green.

The Hue control has a form of built-in selection that can be very useful if you only need to make changes to parts of the picture that are a certain colour. There is a menu near the top of the Hue/Saturation window, and by default this is set to the Master option. This simply means that the Hue control will affect all colours. The menu offers a range of six colours that can be used instead, and changes will then be applied only to the selected colour. Sliders appear on the colour bars to indicate the colour range that will be altered by the Hue, Saturation, and Lightness controls. There are two sets of sliders, with the inner pair indicating the range of colours that will be fully altered by adjustments to the controls. The outer pair indicates the colours that will be affected to a lesser extent.

In Figure 2.68 I have selected Magenta from the menu, which is a good match for the colour of the flower head. Since there is nothing else in the picture that is close to the colour of the flower head, I have moved the sliders further apart in an attempt to ensure that all the relevant colours

Fig.2.69 Both types of colour fringing are apparent here

are embraced. Moving the Hue control to the right has turned the flower head yellow/green in colour, but the rest of the image is unchanged. The Saturation and Lightness controls, like the Hue control, will only affect colours within the selected colour range, so I use them to produce a slightly brighten flower head with stronger colours.

Purple fringing

Purple fringing, or chromatic aberration as it is also known, is a problem that occurs with many cameras. It mainly occurs when photographing something that is very dark when there is a bright background, such as the branches of a tree with bright sky in the background. However, with some cameras it can occur in parts of the image where the contrast is relatively low. There is a thin blue or purple area where the light and dark parts of the image meet, and it is from the purple fringing name is derived. Although it is termed purple fringing, there are usually two fringes, one on each side of the branch (or whatever). There is a blue/purple fringe on one edge and a orange/yellow one on the opposite edge. In practice the other fringe is often much less obvious though.

In the example of Figure 2.69 there is a massive amount of blue/purple down the left-hand side of the wooden post. A highly zoomed view is

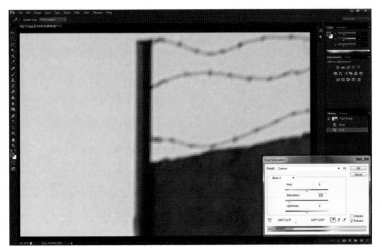

Fig.2.70 The purple fringing has been removed

shown in Figure 2.69 so that it is easy to see the fringing, but it was severe enough to be all too obvious when viewing the entire image on the screen. To remove the purple fringing I launched the Hue/Saturation control, selected Magentas from the menu, and then used the Eyedropper tool at a point on the fringing in order to optimise accuracy. Setting the colour saturation at a low value removed the blue/purple colour and made the left side of the post blend in properly with the rest (Figure 2.70).

In this example the yellow/orange fringing on the opposite side of the post is also fairly prominent. It was removed using the same basic technique, but Yellows was selected from the menu. The Eyedropper tool was then used to sample the fringing and optimise the accuracy of the process. Taking the saturation to a low level then removed the colour, leaving a much more natural looking post (Figure 2.71).

Red-eye reduction

Most digital cameras have a facility to reduce the so-called red-eye effect when taking flash photographs of people using the built-in flashgun. While red-eye reduction features are generally quite effective, they do not guarantee that your photographs will never suffer from this problem. Actually it is not just photographs of people that can fall foul of the red-

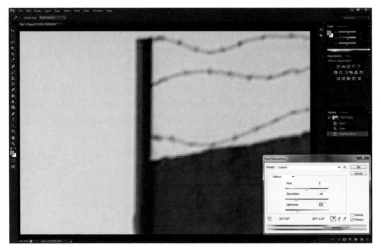

Fig.2.71 The yellow fringing has also been removed

eye effect, and it can occur when photographing, cats, dogs, and many other animals.

It can also happen when the light source is close to the camera, or is shining in the same direction as a light source on the camera. For example, if there is low sunlight coming from behind you, and the subject is just to one side of your shadow, there is a likelihood of the light being reflected off their retinas and back to the camera. Some of the worst cases of red-eye that I have encountered were actually on photographs of animals taken using natural light.

Most photo editing programs have an automatic red-eye reduction facility. In the absence of a human volunteer prepared to be seen in print with glowing red eyes, I have used a photograph of a squirrel for this example (Figure 2.72). Photoshop has an automatic facility for dealing with red-eye in the form of the Red Eye tool. This is grouped with other "healing" tools in the toolbar down the left-hand edge of the screen, and it accessed via the seventh button from the top. Right-click this button and then select Red Eye Tool from the little pop-out menu.

In order to use this tool it is just a matter of dragging a rectangle around the eye you wish to process. Like most automatic red-eye reduction systems, it locates the offending red areas, or other highly coloured areas, and replaces then with black or a very dark grey. This can work quite well, produce odd looking results, or anything in between these two. It

Fig.2.72 The squirrel is suffering from a case of red-eye

has worked reasonably well in Figure 2.73. In many cases it is not totally convincing though, and it is often better if the job is done manually using the Hue control.

Fig.2.73 The red-eye has been removed quite well

Fig.2.74 Here a more subtle approach has been used

Fig.2.75 The finished squirrel photograph

Fig.2.76 The slightly "soft" fox picture zoomed to Actual Pixels

Many of the colours in the photograph are similar to the reds and orange colours in the red-eye area. I therefore used the Magic Lasso tool to select the eye of the squirrel before launching the Hue/Saturation control. This ensures that the changes are only applied to the red-eye and that the rest of the photograph is left untouched. A common approach is to reduce the colour saturation to zero, which removes all the colour from the red-eye area of the image, giving grey-eye rather than red-eye. The lightness control is then backed off so that the grey areas are darkened, but not so much that they become black.

In Figure 2.74 I have tried a different approach. I have adjusted the three slider controls to reduce the colour saturation and brightness, and to change the red eye to a brown one. The OK button was then pressed in order to keep the changes and exit the Hue/Saturation control, and then the selection marquee around the eye was removed. This gave the processed image of Figure 2.75, which perhaps looks a bit more convincing than the effect obtained when simply converting the reds to black, and is certainly less bland.

Sharpening

Digital cameras tend to produce slightly "soft" images due to the way in which they work, and the need for filters to reduce problems with moiré

Fig.2.77 Applying the Sharpen filter has made some improvement

patterns when photographing some types of subject matter. The cameras therefore include built-in sharpening facilities that counteract this "softness". The built-in sharpening may be all that is required, but some additional processing may be needed at times. Also, the best results are not usually obtained by using a lot of in-camera sharpening and then using other forms of processing. If images are likely to receive a fair amount of processing using a photo editing program, results are generally best if little or no in-camera sharpening is used, and the sharpening is applied once all the other processing has been completed.

Some photo editing software, including Photoshop, offers several different types of sharpening, but the basic way in which this effect operates is always the same. Blurring results in light areas producing an increase in the brightness of nearby dark areas, and dark areas causing a reduction in the brightness of nearby light areas. Sharpening effects try to counteract this by providing localised increases in contrast.

Some sharpening facilities have various controls that enable the effect to be optimised for any given image, but getting the best results from this type of thing can be quite difficult. For many purposes a simple automatic system is all that is needed. Photoshop offers three methods that are fully automatic, and two types that are controlled manually.

In order to use the fully automatic method it is merely necessary to load the image into the Photoshop editor and then select Sharpen from the

Fig.2.78 The Sharpen More filter has worked reasonably well here

Sharpen submenu of the Filter menu (Filter-Sharpen-Sharpen). The degree of sharpening provided is not that high, and with some images its effect is often barely noticeable. With others its effect is more noticeable, and all that is needed. Figure 2.76 shows the Photoshop editor loaded with a photograph of a fox resting in the grass. It has been zoomed using the Actual Pixels option from the View menu, which should always be used when assessing the sharpness of an image.

While not totally blurred, it is far from being completely sharp. It was taken through a closed window, and this usually gives a noticeable reduction in contrast. I think that the camera's auto-focusing has focused on the grass just in front of the fox, rather than on the fox itself. Using the Sharpen facility has not made a huge difference (Figure 2.77). In fact with just a quick glance at the two images you might not notice any difference at all, but on closer inspection a small but worthwhile improvement should be evident.

The image is too blurred for a basic quick fix of this type to be successful. A stronger sharpening filter is available from the Sharpen submenu via the Sharpen More option. This has a much stronger effect than the standard Sharpen type, and with many pictures it is too strong and too obvious. In this case it has actually worked quite well (Figure 2.78), and has given a big improvement without going completely "over the top".

Fig.2.79 Here the Sharpen filter has been used three times

It is possible to use the normal Sharpen facility two or more times in order to obtain a greater degree of sharpening. Sharpening has been applied three times in Figure 2.79, and this certainly gives a much sharper looking result, and many people would probably be happy with this version, but there are some odd effects starting to appear in parts of the image. Using the Sharpen command a fourth time (Figure 2.80) has certainly taken things too far, with some odd effects appearing in some of the sharpened highlights.

The normal problem if too much sharpening is applied is the so-called halo effect. If things are taken too far, the boost in local contrast provided by the sharpening tends to produce white lines close to sharpened edges. Other odd effects can be produced, especially in highly textured areas. Dots of bright colours can appear, and this problem is starting to appear in a few places in Figure 2.80.

Adjusting sharpness

Where more than a small amount of sharpening is required it is best to resort to one of the methods that use manual control. One of these is Smart Sharpen, which is an option in the Sharpen submenu (Filter-Sharpen-Smart Sharpen). A new window is launched when this option

Fig.2.80 Using the Sharpen filter four times has produced some odd effects

is selected (Figure 2.81), and the left-hand section shows part of the image at the Actual Pixels zoom level. You can drag the contents of this panel so that it shows the required part of the image.

The applied level of sharpening will be shown in this panel, but it will also be shown on the image in the main editing window if the Preview checkbox is ticked, as it will be by default. It is therefore better to have the Adjust Sharpness window out of the way in one corner of the screen. The main display can then be used to monitor the effects of adjustments to the sharpness controls. Using the Preview facility will slow things down, but with any reasonably modern computer it should not become unacceptably sluggish. Note that the Preview option is usually available when some form of control window appears, and that it is usually best to use this facility where it is available.

A menu enables three types of sharpening to be applied. The Gaussian Blur option gives the standard version of sharpening, and is a good general purpose option. Lens Blur is used when trying to counteract a lack of sharpness due to a slight lack of resolution from the lens, inaccurate focusing, or inadequate depth of field. Inadequate depth of field and slightly inaccurate focusing are probably the main problems with the fox picture. I used the Lens Blur option for this example, but results would probably have been very similar using the Gaussian Blur option. Motion blur is designed to counteract blurring caused by a moving

Fig.2.81 The Smart Sharpen filter gives greater control of the process

subject or "camera shake". This type of blurring will be considered later in this chapter.

The More Accurate checkbox will not be ticked by default. Using this feature gives better performance with very fine detail, which is often an advantage, and it is definitely a good idea to use it with low resolution images, such as those for web pages. The downside of using this feature is that it will tend to increase problems with the sharpening making "noise" in the picture more obvious. "Noise" is the graininess or texture of coloured dots that can sometimes be seen on digital images, especially in plain areas such as expanses of blue sky. It is most severe when using high ISO sensitivities or long shutter speeds. Anyway, if there is a lot of "noise" in an image it might be better to tick this checkbox.

Having selected suitable options, it is then a matter of using the two slider controls to provide the required sharpening effect. The Radius control determines how far the sharpening will extend from edges, and the Amount control sets the degree of sharpening used. In general, a low value of about one is used with small images and those that only need a small amount of sharpening. Higher values are used with images that have large pixel counts and (or) there is a fair amount of fuzziness to contend with. However, in practice it is a matter of trying various Radius settings, and adjusting the Amount control for the best results at each of these settings. The right settings are the ones that you deem to give the best subjective result, regardless of whether they conform to the "rules of the game".

On the face of it, the same amount of sharpening should be needed regardless of how an image will be viewed. In practice it is not as simple as that, and it is generally best to err on the side of caution when sharpening an image that will be viewed on a monitor. Even getting slightly carried away will usually result in an image that looks unnatural and obviously sharpened to excess. Presumably due to the lower contrast of a print, a slightly higher level of sharpening often gives the best result, although it is still necessary to use a degree of restraint in order to avoid unnatural looking images.

In Figure 2.81 I have set the Radius control to a somewhat higher setting than normal and then advanced the Amount control as far as I could without obvious problems becoming evident. This has sharpened the fur on the front of fox's head without producing some of the odd effects that occurred using the ordinary Sharpen command. Some parts of the image look obviously over-sharpened with the image viewed on a monitor, but it would probably look fine on a large print.

Motion Blur

Motion blur is cause by movement of the camera or the subject while the exposure is being made. It is not usually a problem when using fast shutter speeds and a wide-angle or standard lens. It becomes more problematic with slow shutter speeds, with powerful telephoto lenses, and when taking close-ups. Modern cameras often have built-in image stabilisation, or use lenses that sport this feature. This reduces the risk of camera shake, but at best you can only go three or four shutter speeds lower before camera shake becomes a problem.

For example, if you would otherwise need to use a shutter speed of one hundredth of a second or faster, with image stabilisation you might be able to get away with $1/15^{th}$ or $1/8^{th}$ of a second. Of course, image stabilisation does not help with any movement within the picture. In fact it encourages the use of slower shutter speeds which greatly increase the chances of blurring due to movement of the subject matter.

Anyway, the Motion Blur setting of the Smart Sharpen facility can help with this type of blurring, but only in minor cases. With severe motion blurring, especially if it gives a double-image effect, there is no effective way of counteracting the blurring. Using this version of the Smart Sharpen

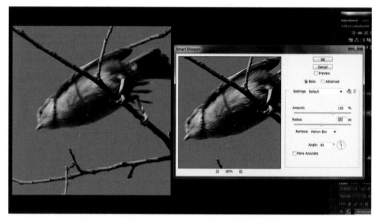

Fig.2.82 The Motion option has helped to sharpen this image

facility it much the same as normal, but there is an additional control for the angle of the blurring. You should find that varying the angle produces little effect at some settings and a stronger effect at others. The angle that produces the strongest effect is the one to use.

If the angle control has little effect, either the problem is due to motion blur, or the degree of blur is too great for the sharpening to be of any help. In Figure 2.82 the Preview facility is switched off so that you can compare the original image with the sharpened version in the Smart Sharpen window.

Unsharp Mask

Unsharp Mask is a more complicated form of sharpening, and a highly regarded one. It has three controls (Figure 2.83) in place of the two in the Smart Sharpening facility. It is accessed by selecting Unsharp Mask from the Sharpen submenu (Filter-Sharpen-Unsharp Mask). The top control is used to set the required amount of sharpening, and the middle control is the familiar radius type.

The third slider control sets the Threshold, which is the difference needed between pixels before the sharpening will be applied. Here we are talking in terms of the difference in contrast needed before it will be accepted as an edge and sharpened. High values result in Photoshop finding few areas to sharpen. With a low value the filtering is applied almost

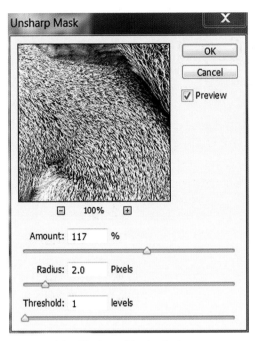

Fig.2.83 The Unsharp Mask window

everywhere on the image, which usually results in patterns of dots starting to emerge from previously plain areas of the image. It can take a fair amount of juggling with the three controls in order to obtain the best results, but it should be possible to obtain a reasonably sharp looking picture provided the original image contains an adequate amount of detail. Figures 2.84 and 2.85 show "before" and "after" images that show the effect of Unsharp Mask filtering.

Lens Correction

Photoshop has a facility that is designed to compensate for deficiencies in the lens of a camera. It is accessed using the Lens Correction option in the Filter menu (Filter-Lens Correction). The photograph of Figure 2.86 has a common problem called vignetting, which is the darkening in the corners of the picture. This is something that occurs to some extent with any camera lens, but it is normally kept down to a low enough level to be of no importance. However, with some types of lens it is quite noticeable.

The types of lens that are most prone to this problem are very wide-angle types, and zoom lenses that cover a massive zoom range. Older wide-angle lenses when used on a digital camera will often produce this problem in a quite severe form. As one would probably expect, it is more likely to occur with a cheap camera and lens than when using upmarket professional camera equipment. It also tends to be more of a problem with digital cameras than with film types.

Fig.2.84 The "before" picture of the raven is slightly "soft"

Fig.2.85 Unsharp mask filtering has been quite effective

Fig.2.86 This photograph has very noticeable vignetting

It is easily corrected using the two vignette controls in the Lens Correction facility, but on selecting this option the automatic version will be shown

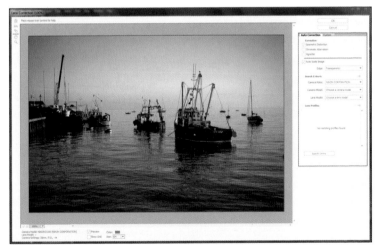

Fig.2.87 The Auto Correction tab is used by default

Fig.2.88 The vignetting has been corrected manually

by default (Figure 2.87). This facility is very useful if you use one of the supported lens and camera combinations, and it will then deal with various lens problems fully automatically, or with minimal manual adjustment. However, correcting vignetting manually is quite quick and easy if you are using equipment for which there is no suitable lens profile available.

Operate the Custom tab near the top right-hand corner of the window to switch into the manual adjustment mode (Figure 2.88). The two Vignette controls are in the middle section of the control panel on the right. Moving the Amount slider to the right lightens the corners, but it might not be possible to find a setting that gives an even level of brightness across the frame. However, it should be possible to obtain reasonably consistent results by adjusting the Midpoint slider, but this will probably require a certain amount of experimentation. It is possible to deliberately add vignetting by moving the Amount slider to the left. This effect is often used as a means of concentrating the viewer's attention on the subject matter in the centre of the picture, and distracting them from the background. It is an effect that was often used with portraits in the early days of photography, and it can be used to give a picture an olde worlde look.

Fig.2.89 This woodland scene suffers from converging verticals

Fig.2.90 The Vertical Perspective control has been used here to straighten the picture

Converging verticals

The perspective controls can be used to introduce perspective effects, and they are also useful for correcting a problem known as converging verticals. This problem occurs most commonly when photographing tall buildings. The camera is normally aimed upwards in order to avoid having an excessive amount of foreground and too little building in the shot. This tends to produce a photograph that gives the impression the building is keeling over. The cause of the problem is a standard perspective effect. With the tops of the buildings being much further away than the lower stories, they are smaller and closer together.

In Figure 2.89 the two trees in the foreground show this effect, and they seem to be leaning toward one another. While the two trees were not bolt upright, they were not leaning over in the manner suggested by the photograph. Using the Vertical perspective control it is possible to expand the upper part of the picture and straighten the trees (Figure 2.90). Unfortunately, this horizontal stretching of the picture results in an increasing amount of cropping towards the top.

Fig.2.91 This picture is exhibiting pincushion distortion

Distortion

The Distortion control is used to correct pincushion or barrel distortion. The photograph shown in Figure 2.91 is suffering from a very obvious case of pincushion distortion. Note how the horizon is far from straight. It curves inwards towards the centre of the picture, which is pincushion distortion. If it curved outwards from the centre it would be barrel distortion. By moving the Distortion slider to the left it is possible to correct pincushion distortion (Figure 2.92). Move it to the right in order to counteract barrel distortion. It is useful to tick the Grid checkbox before trying to correct any distortion problems. The horizontal grid lines give you something to compare the wonky horizon with, and make it much easier to straighten things out.

The distortion facilities are primarily included as a means of correcting problems with lenses, but they can also be used to deliberately distort an image. In Figure 2.94 for example, the bee photograph of Figure 2.93 has been deliberately distorted to produce a sort of fisheye lens effect. When used for correcting lens problems you may find that you only use this facility with one lens, and that more or less the same settings are used each time. Rather than starting with the default settings, it is

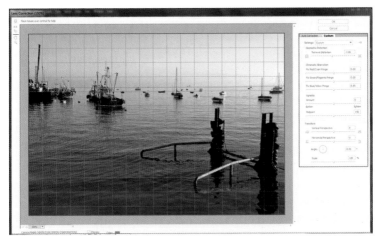

Fig.2.92 Using the Distortion slider has cured the problem

then best to use the Previous Correction option from the small pop-down menu near the top right-hand corner of the window.

Fig.2.93 The original version of the bee photograph

Fig.2.94 The deliberately distorted version of the bee photograph

There are controls for fixing problems with red-eye and various types of colour fringing. I have had mixed results with these, but they offer a quick and easy solution in cases where they work well. The alternative methods offered by Photoshop can be used in cases where the required improvement is not obtained.

Black and White

Photoshop has two facilities for converting a colour image to black and white, and the simpler of the two is the Desaturate option (Image – Adjustments– Desaturate). It simply uses an average of the colour values for each pixel, which in some cases might be all that is needed. This is actually the same as setting the Saturation control to zero, as described earlier (see Figure 2.22).

Using this method on the insect photograph of Figure 2.95 produced the passable result of Figure 2.96. The insect stands out reasonably well from the background, but overall the image is perhaps a little on the dark side. However, if deemed necessary, this could easily be adjusted using the various forms of brightness and contrast control available in Photoshop. The Curves facility for example, works more or less normally with black and white images.

A potential problem with the simple approach to black and white conversion is that it can produce rather bland results. Suppose that a

Fig.2.95 The colour version of the insect photograph

picture of a vase of flowers is converted into black and white, and that the flowers are various colours but are all in the mid-tone range. In the

Fig.2.96 The desaturated black and white version

Fig.2.97 Simple desaturation has not worked too well in this case

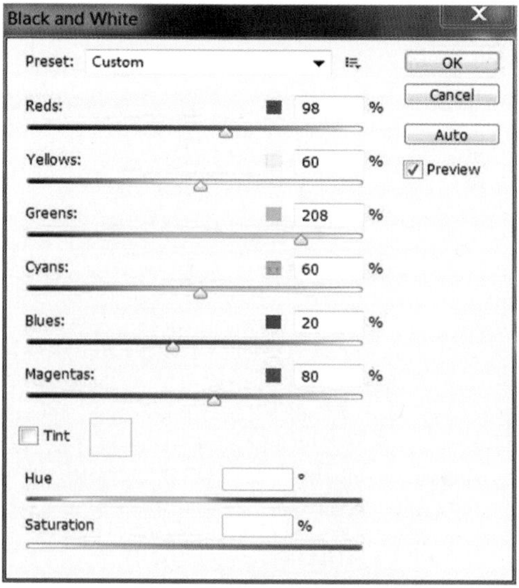

Black and White

Preset: Custom

Reds: 98   %

Yellows: 60   %

Greens: 208   %

Cyans: 60   %

Blues: 20   %

Magentas: 80   %

Tint

Hue   °

Saturation   %

OK
Cancel
Auto
✓ Preview

Fig.2.98 The Black and White window

black and white version they will all be a mid grey and will all look much the same. A better result would probably be obtained by weighting the conversion so that some colours were converted to relatively dark tones while others were made lighter than normal. This would give viewers the impression that the flowers were different colours, and would give a more lively and interesting picture.

Figure 2.97 shows a simple black and

Fig.2.99 Altering the colour levels has produced a better result

white conversion of the colour picture featured earlier in Figure 2.54. The blue and orange ropes have tremendous colour contrast in the original version, but they are practically the same shade of grey in the converted version. Photoshop provides a sophisticated form of black and white conversion in the form of its Black and White feature (Image-Adjustments-Black and White). This has slider controls that enable the relative strengths of the colours to be controlled (Figure 2.98). In the black and white conversion of Figure 2.99 I have made the blues darker and the yellow/red colours lighter. This has made the bright blue rope darker and brought out some more texture in it, and made the orange rope lighter so that it contrasts better with the blue rope.

Another potential problem with a basic black and white conversion is that bright colours can be translated into rather drab shades of grey. The photograph of Figure 2.100 has some very bright greens produced by the sun shining through the leaves on the tree. Unfortunately, in the simple conversion to black and white of Figure 2.101 the effect of the light coming through the leaves has been lost, as has the mood of the original picture. In the version of Figure 2.102 I have increased the green level, which has duly lightened the leaves and regained some of the mood of the original image. I also increased the red level slightly which should have lightened the fallen leaves in the foreground that are catching the sunlight.

Fig.2.100 The leaves in this photograph look very bright

Fig.2.101 The monochrome leaves are rather subdued

Fig.2.102 The leaves are much brighter in this version

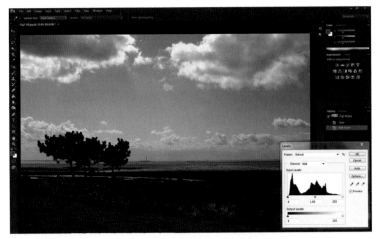

Fig.2.103 The Levels window includes a histogram

Levels

Using the Levels feature to make automatic adjustments was covered previously (page 51), but in order to get the most from this facility it is necessary to use manual control. As can be seen from Figure 2.103, choosing Levels from the Adjustments submenu produces a window that includes a histogram. A histogram that shows the strengths of the individual colour channels can be obtained by selecting Histogram from the Window menu on the menu bar, but the one featured here is a more basic type that shows combined luminance levels. If you are not familiar with this type of histogram, it should perhaps be explained that the horizontal axis covers a range of brightness levels from black on the extreme left to white on the extreme right. The heights of the bars show the relative number of pixels at each luminance level.

This histogram is actually more than just a histogram, and it includes controls that permit the contrast and brightness of the image to be altered. There are two sets of slider controls, and the lower set controls the maximum and minimum luminosity. Dark grey can be set as the minimum level instead of black by moving the left-hand slider to the right. Similarly, light grey rather than white can be set as the maximum level by moving the right hand slider to the left. Reductions in contrast of this type are not often needed, but some subjects can benefit from this treatment. Some printing processes require a reduction in contrast of this type to prevent large dark areas from printing as solid areas of black.

Fig.2.104 The brightened version of the picture

The upper set of sliders is of greater use to most users. If the slider at the white end is moved inwards, areas that were previously light grey become white, and the lower levels of luminosity are shuffled upwards.

Fig.2.105 The colour saturation has been increased

Adjusting the slider at the other end produces a similar effect with dark greys becoming black and higher levels of luminosity being shuffled downwards. Neither type of adjustment is normally applied to a picture that already has a full range of tones. Doing so would result in clipping. The idea is to move the sliders inwards so that they match the lightest and darkest tones present in the image, as indicated by the histogram. This gives the full contrast range from the image.

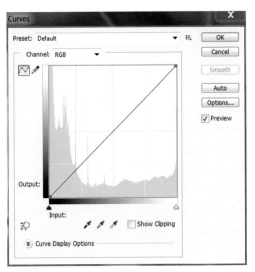

Fig.2.106 The Curves window

Fig.2.107 Here the straight line has been dragged into a curve

Fig.2.108 Here a reduction in brightness has been provided

The photograph in Figure 2.103 is very dark and seems to be underexposed, and the large peak towards the left of the histogram seems to confirm this. However, there seems to be a lack of pixels at the highest and lowest luminance levels, so it is not a classic case of over or under exposure. It is generally too dark though, with a large number of pixels at low levels of luminance and very few at the high end. Looking at the photograph itself, the dark green grass should clearly be much lighter.

I moved the two sliders inward slightly to match up with the lightest and darkest tones present in the image to optimise contrast. The upper set of slider controls includes an additional control in the middle. This is a very useful tool and it is the one that usually matters most when using the Levels facility to edit a light or dark image. It can be used to bring out details that are tending to disappear in dark areas of the image. A general increase in brightness will lighten an image, but lightest areas of the picture will usually be clipped. Using a simple brightness control to darken an over-bright image will tend to clip areas of very low luminance.

Better results are obtained by moving the middle slider control to the left to brighten an image, or to the right to darken it. The tone selected using this control becomes the new mid-tone, and the others are moved up or down to accommodate this change. In this example it is an adjustment to the left to brighten the picture that is needed (Figure 2.104).

Fig.2.109 More than one control point can be used

This has lightened the image but has not caused any clipping and loss of highlight detail. Unfortunately, as is often the case, it has produced very weak colours. However, increasing the colour saturation using the Saturation and Vibrance controls produced a big improvement (Figure 2.105).

Curves

The Curves facility has similar features to the Levels facility, but it is even more versatile. The Levels dialogue box has a single slider for controlling mid tones, but the Curves window effectively provides numerous controls that can be used to mould the contrast and brightness precisely as required. When the Curves window is opened there is a noticeable lack of curves. Instead, there is a graph that has a straight line going from the bottom left-hand corner to the top right-hand corner (Figure 2.106). What is the graph showing? It simply shows the input levels on the horizontal scale versus the output levels on the vertical scale.

As things stand, each input level produces an identical output level, and no processing is applied. The line can be dragged into a curve, as in Figure 2.107, and this alters the relationship between the input and output values. The zero and 100 percent input levels still produce zero and 100

Fig.2.110 Complex curves can produce some odd effects

percent output levels, but changes occur at other levels. The readout near the bottom left-hand corner of the window shows that there is a 62 percent input level and a 34 percent output level at the point where the line was dragged. Lower values give higher brightness, so dragging the line in this direction produces an increase in brightness without introducing significant clipping. Dragging the line in the opposite direction, as in Figure 2.108 gives a reduction in brightness. It is actually the image of Figure 2.18 that is being processed here.

It is possible to obtain input and output values for any point on the line by first moving the pointer away from the line so that an ordinary arrow pointer is obtained. Then hold down the left mouse button and move the pointer along the line. The readout will show the input and output levels for the current position of the pointer, and it will automatically update as the pointer is moved. Just place the pointer anywhere on the line while still holding down the left mouse button and the readout will show the corresponding input and output levels.

Using one point on the graph line gives a little more control than the Levels method, but not much more. Greater control can be obtained by dragging other points on the line, which gives more control points. Suppose that you needed to make the butterfly photograph darker, but would like to apply the darkening to only the mid and low luminance

Fig.2.111 A sepia tint has been added to this picture

parts of the picture, with the lighter parts being left unaltered. First a point is placed on the line at about the 25 percent input/output level. This is done to effectively anchor the lower part of the line in place so that it is not influenced by adjustments made higher up. With the first point in place the upper part of the line is then dragged upward (Figure 2.109). The darker parts of the picture have been made darker, but there is no change to the lightest parts of the image. This has left it with a bright and summery feel, while putting a bit more colour back into the darker but previously overexposed and faded looking areas.

It is possible to have up to 16 points on the line, which effectively provide separate brightness controls for various bands of luminance values. Odd effects can be obtained by using complex curves, as in the example of Figure 2.110. In most cases two or three control points and some fairly simple curves are all that will be needed.

Dragging the bottom of the line upward reduces the maximum level to a shade of grey rather than white. Moving the top of the line downward gives a shade of grey instead of white as the minimum level. This is the same as adjusting the lower set of slider controls in the Levels window, and it reduces contrast. Moving the top and bottom of the line inward is equivalent to using the upper set of slider controls in the Levels window, and it increases contrast.

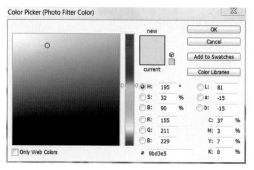

Fig.2.112 The Color Picker window

In common with the Levels window, the Curves window includes a Channel menu that permits each primary colour to be adjusted separately. With both facilities this gives tremendous control over the colour balance, but it is not exactly an easy way of adjusting the colours. It is probably of more use for special effects than it is for everyday adjustments of colour balance.

There are two buttons near the top left-hand corner of the graph, and the one on the left is used by default. The button on the right (like a pencil) gives an alternative method of controlling the graph line. The line can be drawn onto the graph when this freehand mode is used. It is not necessary to draw a complete line, and Photoshop will merge the section you draw with the existing line. Having drawn a line, you can revert to the original mode and move the control points in the normal way.

Tints

Converting colour images to black and white ones was covered previously, but suppose you require a toned monochrome print such as a sepia type. Adding a tint to a monochrome image using Photoshop is very easy, but note that the picture must be in a colour mode and not a greyscale type. If necessary, convert the image to a colour type by selecting Image-Mode-RGB Color from the menu system. A tint can then be added using the Photo Filter facility (Image-Adjustments-Photo Filter). A range of preset filter types are available from the menu in the Photo Filter window, and the Density slider control enables the strength of the filtering to be adjusted. In Figure 2.111 the Sepia filter has been used.

You can use a filter of any desired colour by operating the Color radio button and then left-clicking on the coloured square just to its right. This brings up the Color Picker (Figure 2.112) window where the required colour is selected. Bear in mind that the Density control is still available

Fig.2.113 Here the selected blue tint has been added to the picture

when you select a custom filter colour, so it is the maximum strength that you are selecting. Weaker tinting using the same colour can be obtained via the density control. In Figure 2.113 a blue tint has been added. Of

Fig.2.114 Warm filtering has been added to the colour version of the image

Fig.2.115 This is a true black and white image with no grey levels

course, the filtering is not restricted to black and white images. In Figure 2.114 warm up filtering has been added to the colour version of the image used in the black and white examples.

Threshold

Threshold is another command in the Adjustments submenu (Image-Adjustments-Threshold). Although images are often referred to as "black and white" types, in most cases this is not really an accurate description. They are mostly greyscale types that have black areas, white areas, and a range of greys between these two extremes. Using the Threshold command provides a true conversion to black and white. In other words, dark areas of the picture are converted to black, light areas are converted to white, and there are no shades of grey in between.

In Figure 2.115 a colour picture of a squirrel has been given the true black and white treatment. A histogram of the image is provided, and there is a slider control immediately beneath it. This is used to set the required threshold level. Pixels at or above this threshold level are made white, and those below it are made black. A fairly high setting will often bring out textures much better than a lower one, but can make the image very dark overall. The threshold level then has to be a compromise that

Fig.2.116 Some of the filter effects do not have a preview facility

shows some detail but does not make the picture too dark and dreary. For an interesting alternative to the standard effect, the black and white areas can be transposed by using the Invert command (Image-Adjustments-Invert) on the processed image.

Filters

Photoshop has a wide range of effects filters that can be accessed via the Filter menu or via the Filter Gallery. Starting with the filters in the Filter menu and its submenus, selecting one of these will sometimes result in a preset effect being applied to the image, but in most cases a dialogue box of some sort will appear on the screen. This will permit one or more adjustments to be made, and there will often be a panel that previews part of the processed image. However, in some cases there is no form of preview facility, as in the Extrude example of Figure 2.116. You then have to use some likely settings, apply the filtering (Figure 2.117), then undo the filtering and try again if you are not satisfied with the result.

The Filter Gallery is activated by selecting the Filter Gallery option from the Filter menu (Filter-Filter Gallery). This brings up a large window that has three sections (Figure 2.118). On the left there is a large preview panel, the various filters are accessed via the middle section, and the

Fig.2.117 The Extrude filtering applied to the butterfly image

controls for the selected filter are provided in the right-hand section. Stained Glass filtering is being used in the example of Figure 2.118.

There is insufficient space available here for a detailed discussion of the various filters, but this would probably be pointless anyway. The best way to learn about the filter effects is to load in a photograph and then experiment with them. Where there are controls that enable the filtering to be adjusted, try various settings to see what happens. Some of the best filter effects are produced by accident rather than design.

Noise

The Filter menu has a Noise submenu, and most of the options on offer here are concerned with the removal of noise rather than adding it for effect. Noise is not usually a problem, but it can be noticeable when using high ISO sensitivities and (or) long exposures. Digital cameras often have built-in facilities for reducing problems with noise, and you might prefer to use these rather than trying to deal with the problem later using Photoshop.

Fig.2.118 Here the Stained Glass filter is being used

There are two types of noise that affect digital photographs, which are luminance and colour noise, which is also known as "chroma" noise. Luminance noise is where there is a random grainy pattern in plain areas with some pixels being much lighter or darker than the others. Colour noise also produces a grainy pattern in plain areas, but with some of the pixels being the wrong colour. In many cases these pixels will be very brightly coloured, and colour noise tends to be much more noticeable than the luminance variety. The two are not mutually exclusive, and one type of noise will usually be accompanied by the other, but one will probably be much more severe than the other.

The Despeckle filter (Filter-Noise-Despeckle) can be used to reduce luminance noise. It works by looking for edges in an image, and then slightly blurring everything else. Unfortunately, it will tend to blur any speckled part of the image, whether the differences in luminance are due to noise or form a legitimate part of the image. Noise reduction systems always involve a trade-off between reducing noise and preserving detail in the image.

The Reduce Noise filter (Filter-Noise-Reduce Noise) is useful for reducing colour noise. In the example of Figure 2.119 the photograph has been underexposed. Lightening and sharpening it has produced a mild but significant problem with noise, as can be seen in the magnified main

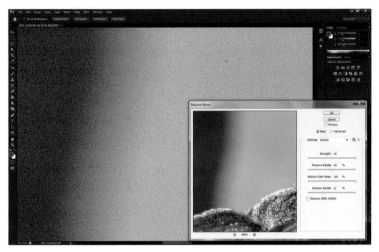

Fig.2.119 Filtering can be used to reduce noise

view of the image. The sliders are used to control the amount of colour noise reduction, the amount of detail that is preserved, the degree of sharpening applied to the surviving details, and the strength of the noise reduction. This is a subjective matter, and the user has to make his or her own decision over the best compromise between noise reduction and the preservation of detail.

Selections
and Layers

Cropping

Cropping is where the picture is trimmed at one or more of the edges, and it is one of the most common forms of photo editing. Many cameras have viewfinders that show rather less than actually appears in the photographs, and this even applies to some quite expensive SLR and DSLR cameras. Consequently, it is often necessary to trim the edges of the image in order to get back to your original composition. Another reason for cropping pictures is that you were not as careful as you might have been when originally framing the shot. Some careful cropping at the editing stage will often make up for some careless framing when taking the shot.

Sometimes you are simply unable to get close enough to the subject, and even with maximum zoom it is something less than frame filling. This is often the case with wildlife and sports photography, and when at an event photographing celebrities. Cropping the edges of the photograph effectively extends the zoom range of your camera and gets you closer to the action. It is often the case that there are scenes within scenes, and particularly with wide-angle photography, it is often possible to produce several pictures simply by using different crops of the same shot.

Of course, there is a downside to cropping images, and this is the resultant reduction in the number of pixels. This is unlikely to be of great importance when trimming small amounts of extraneous material from the edges of photographs, but it can limit the maximum print size if a substantial part of the original image is discarded. Many modern cameras have sensors with well over 10 million pixels, which in theory means that you could crop about half the picture and still produce a reasonable A3 size print. No doubt this is possible with some cameras, but bear in mind that it is not just the number of pixels that is important. The image

Fig.3.1 This photograph would benefit from slight cropping

must be sharp and have a reasonably low noise level if it is to produce a high quality print.

The photograph in Figure 3.1 is not bad as it stands but the 3:2 aspect ratio of the camera is not ideally suited to the subject matter. There are some distracting leaves in the foreground on the right edge of the picture, and a distracting stem and leaf in the background near the opposite edge. A better image can be produced by cropping the picture to remove or reduce these parts of the picture.

A Crop option is available in the Image menu, and this can be used in conjunction with the rectangular selection tool, but cropping is much easier using the Crop tool. This is the fifth one from the top in the toolbar at the left-hand edge of the screen. To use it you simply drag a rectangle that covers the part of the image that you wish to retain. Alternatively, with the CS6 version of the Crop tool the control handles appear on the corners and edges of the image as soon as this tool is selected. You can therefore crop the image by simply dragging the edges of the cropping frame using these handles.

In Figure 3.2 I have dragged a rectangle onto the picture and then used the handles to "fine tune" the cropping frame. It is easy to see which parts of the picture will be cropped, as these are shown much darker than the rest of the picture. The selection can be dragged to a new

Fig.3.2 The parts that will be cropped are shown darker than the rest of the image

Fig.3.3 The cropped version of the poppy photograph

Fig.3.4 This photograph would be better in portrait format

position by using any part of it other than the handles. Right-click on the image and select Crop from the pop-up menu, or press the Return key to actually go ahead and crop the picture (Figure 3.3). Right-click and select Cancel to remove the selection, or simply press the Escape key.

In Figure 3.2 some compositional guide lines are displayed in the cropping frame. Various types of guide can be selected via one of the drop-down menus in the bar above the display area, but it is not compulsory to use any guides. Further options in this menu enable them to always be shown, never be shown, or used in an automatic mode. The latter automatically displays the selected type of guide when adjustments are being made, but switches them off at other times. Unless you really find the guides useful it is probably best to switch them off.

Another menu enables the cropping frame to be constrained to a standard aspect ratio such as 4:3, or you can create and save a custom preset ratio if a non-standard type is required. This is useful if (say) you need to crop the picture so that it will exactly fit a common size of printing paper. The small button with the "sun" icon provides some useful controls via another drop-down menu. The opacity of the picture outside the cropping frame can be varied from normal to fully black via a pop-down slider control. By default, the CS6 version of the Crop tool automatically centres

Fig.3.5 The cropped version of the photograph

the cropping frame in the display area, which can be a bit confusing if you are used to the old (static) version. The automatic centring can be switched off via this menu.

Fig.3.6 A high resolution picture of a grass snake

Upright composition

A common compositional error when taking photographs of a predominantly vertical subject is to stick with the usual landscape format rather than turning the camera through ninety degrees and using the portrait format. The photograph in Figure 3.4 works reasonably well despite the vertical nature of the main subject matter, but it can be easily cropped down to the portrait format (Figure 3.5), which perhaps works a bit better than the original. Cropping from landscape to portrait format results in a huge loss of pixels, with typically about half the pixels being discarded. This significantly reduces the maximum usable print size, so it is definitely better to shoot in the portrait format in the first place rather than trying to correct matters later.

Of course, the resolution of modern digital cameras is often very high, and in some cases runs into the tens of millions of pixels. Provided the final image needs to have a more modest resolution it is possible to heavily crop the original image and still obtain an image of good technical quality. The photograph of Figure 3.6 has around 20 million pixels in its original form, but for reproduction in this book the number of pixels had to be reduced to around one million pixels due to the relatively small print size. In terms of area this means that the image could be cropped

Fig.3.7 This highly cropped version still has sufficient resolution for a small print

to about five percent of its original size and still be printed here at full resolution with no reduction in quality.

In its original form (Figure 3.6) this "grab shot" of a grass snake is not totally without merit, but is does not really work all that well either. With massive cropping it can be greatly improved, as in the version of Figure 3.7 which concentrates on the snakes head as it looks out from between the leaves. This has far more impact than the original image, and despite the massive amount of cropping it still has sufficient resolution to be printed properly here. Images for use on the Internet often have a resolution of around 100 to 600 thousand pixels, and an even greater amount of cropping can then be used.

Resizing

Sometimes it is necessary to resize a picture so that it is a certain size in pixels. These days it is usually resizing in a downwards direction that is required, so that a many megapixel photo can fit into (say) a 400 by 300 pixel space on a web page. In order to scale an image up or down, select Image Size from the Image menu (Image-Image Size). This brings

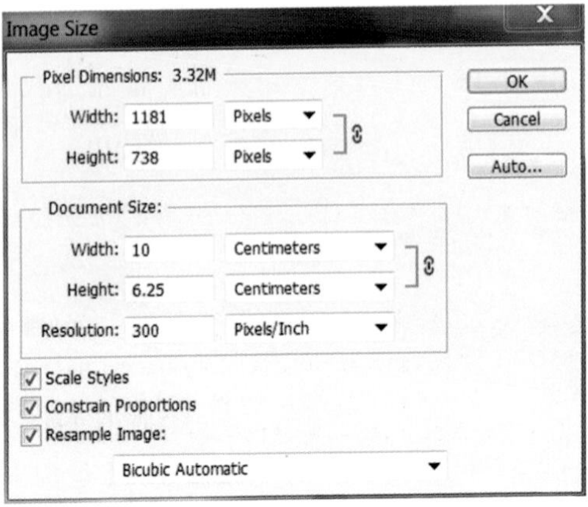

Image Size

Pixel Dimensions: 3.32M

Width: 1181 Pixels ▼ ⎤⑧
Height: 738 Pixels ▼ ⎦

Document Size:

Width: 10 Centimeters ▼ ⎤⑧
Height: 6.25 Centimeters ▼ ⎦
Resolution: 300 Pixels/Inch ▼

OK
Cancel
Auto...

☑ Scale Styles
☑ Constrain Proportions
☑ Resample Image:

Bicubic Automatic ▼

Fig.3.8 The Image Size dialogue box

up the dialogue box of Figure 3.8, where the Resample Image checkbox must be ticked. It is also a good idea to have the Constrain Proportions checkbox ticked. It is tempting to simply set the required width and height for the picture, even if this means changing its aspect ratio, and this is possible if Constrain Proportions checkbox is not ticked. Unfortunately, changes in the aspect ratio often produce some odd looking pictures, so it is better to crop the picture to the desired aspect ratio first, and then resize it.

The required new size for the image is set by entering the appropriate figure into the Pixel Width or Height textbox. You only have to enter one figure, because the program will automatically calculate and enter the other figure. There is a menu at the bottom of the Image Size window that offers various resizing algorithms. The ones that are of most interest are the algorithms that are optimised for enlargement, reduction, and smooth gradients. The latter is good for something like portraits where there are gradual changes in skin tones, or landscapes where there are subtle variations in the sky. With everything set correctly, operate the OK button and the image will be rescaled.

If you need to change the size of the picture so that it will print out at a particular size, go to the Image Size window as before, but make sure that the Resample checkbox is not ticked. Then set the required size in the Document Width or Height textbox. This will change the notional size of the picture, but it will not alter the number of pixels. Bear in mind that there are usually various sizing and scaling options available when the Print facility is used. For example, if you wish to print the photograph as large as possible on the selected paper size, there is usually a "print to fit paper" option that will do this. You do not necessarily have to bother with changes to the notional size of the picture in order to print it at the required size.

Rotation

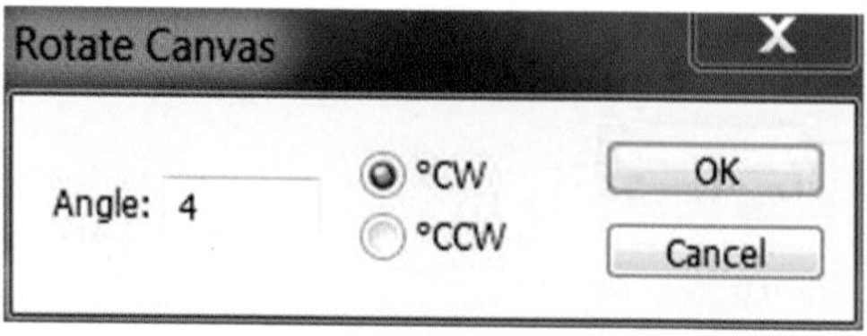

In the Image menu there are a number of rotation options in the Image Rotatation submenu (Image-Image Rotation). The first three of

Rotate Canvas ✕

Angle: 4   ◉ °CW   [OK]
           ○ °CCW [Cancel]

Fig.3.9 The Rotate Canvas window

these rotate the image 90 degrees clockwise or counter-clockwise, and by 180 degrees. Sometimes the image from a digital camera or scanner will need one of these options in order to produce an image that has the correct orientation. The fourth option enables the image to be rotated by an arbitrary amount. In other words, you can specify the degree of rotation and the direction. The small window of Figure 3.9 appears when the Arbitrary option is selected (Image-Image Rotation-Arbitrary). Note that you are not restricted to an integer value, and rotation by (say) 2.5 degrees is permissible. It is therefore possible to rotate the image with a high degree of precision, provided it has suitably high resolution. The Left and Right radio buttons respectively give counter-clockwise and clockwise rotation.

Fig.3.10 The horizon is higher on the left than on the right

*Fig.3.11 A small amount of counter clockwise rotation has
        straightened the horizon*

Arbitrary rotation can be used creatively, but its main use is to correct sloping horizons and similar image faults. The photograph of Figure 3.10 has a fairly obvious sloping horizon, which is made all the more obvious because the horizon is very near the top of the picture. To correct this type of fault the appropriate radio button must be operated so that the image is rotated in the right direction, and you have to guess the correct amount of rotation. Initially there is a tendency to overestimate the amount of rotation required. In most cases only about one degree or so is needed.

As can be seen from the "straightened" version Figure 3.11, Photoshop automatically increases the size of the canvas so that it fully accommodates the rotated image. This leaves four blank areas that must be cropped or retouched. Cropping is quicker and easier, but some content near the edges of the frame will be lost.

The new version of the Crop tool provides another means of rotating the image, and for most purposes this is a more convenient way of handling things. The image of Figure 3.12 has a more obvious problem than the previous example. In Figure 3.13 I have first selected the Crop tool from the toolbar, and then the Grid cropping guide via the relevant drop-down menu. In this case the eight handles around the image are ignored, and instead it is a matter of dragging anywhere outside the image area but

Fig.3.12 *This picture also has a problem with the horizon*

within the display area. Just drag the image round so that the horizon in the photograph is aligned with the nearest horizontal grid lines. With the picture given a suitable degree of rotation it is just a matter of operating the Enter key to make the change take effect (Figure 3.14).

Fig.3.13 *The Crop tool enables the image to be rotated*

Fig.3.14 The rotated version of the image also has the blank areas cropped, but some of the image is also lost

Note that with this method the canvas is enlarged to accommodate the rotated image, but the default is for the four blank areas to be cropped together with some sections at the edges of the image. Obviously this factor is of no importance if you would simply crop the blank areas anyway, and you are quite happy to lose some material at the edges of the image. In fact it is advantageous as it removes the need to tidy up the image by cropping it a second time. It is less satisfactory if you intend to retain everything in the picture and use cloning techniques to fill in the gaps. However, you can manually adjust the cropping frame before going ahead and cropping the image, so you prevent anything vital from being removed.

A variation on rotation using the Crop tool is available via the Straighten button in the options bar. With this button active it is possible to straighten a horizon by simply dragging a line along the horizon. Photoshop will then rotate the image to make the line horizontal. This method works equally well if there is something in the image that is keeling over slightly when it should be vertical. Drag the line along the wonky edge and Photoshop will then rotate the image to make it perfectly vertical.

A third method of rotation is available from the Edit menu, but it is first necessary to select the entire image (Select-All). Then the Rotate option

Fig.3.15 Using the Rotate option from the Edit menu

is selected via the Edit menu (Edit-Transform-Rotate). If you require grid lines they must be switched on using the normal menu system (View-Show-Grid). This method can be used to display grid lines on any image incidentally. It is then just a matter of dragging the image for the required degree of rotation using the same method as for the Crop tool (Figure 3.15). It should be noted that with this method the image will be cropped to some extent, because the canvas will not be enlarged to accommodate the increased size of the image (Figure 3.15). However, this still leaves four triangular blank areas (Figure 3.16).

Ruler tool

An interesting method of rotation is available from the Ruler tool. First select the entire image (Select-All) and then use the Ruler tool to drag a line on the image. The Ruler is hidden under the Eyedropper tool, and is selected by right-clicking the Eyedropper button and then selecting Ruler Tool from the pop-out menu. Using the Rotate command in the Edit menu will result in the image being rotated by an amount equal to the angle of this line.

Note that this does not work in the same way as the Straighten feature of the Crop tool, and trying to use it in that fashion would actually double the slope of the horizon!

Fig.3.16 Parts of the image are cropped and there are four blank areas

I am not sure how this method of rotation could be used to good effect in practice, but it is there if you need it. The Ruler tool can be used to measure the angle and distance of the line drawn on the screen, which is its main function. These are both shown on the Options bar, which in this case is more of an information bar.

The rotation commands are not just for straightening horizons. If you find people have puzzled looks on their faces as they turn one of your photographs this way and that, it probably needs a bit of rotation! You can also use rotation to deliberately slant an image for effect. Either way, the Crop tool is a good choice as it enables the image to be freely rotated and the desired result is obtained, and it then automatically crops the blank areas of the rotated image.

Retouching

Photoshop Elements has brush tools that can be used to retouch photographs using traditional techniques, but this will usually be doing it the hard way. The Clone Stamp tool is almost invariably a much quicker, easier and better way of handling things. It excels at painting over unwanted objects or blemishes by copying from surrounding areas. With a rotated image it can be used to fill in the blank areas by copying nearby material into them.

Figure 3.17 The "before" version of the image

This method has been used in Figure 3.17, which is the finished version of Figure 3.16. The image was rotated using the Arbitrary method, so nothing has been cropped from the original image in Figure 3.16, and nothing has been removed in Figure 3.17 either. Rather than cropping the blank areas they have been filled in using the Clone Stamp tool. This obviously requires some guesswork since there is no way of knowing what should be in the blank areas.

The added sea and sky detail was not much of a problem because these are fairly bland parts of the image. Things like the bowsprit and rigging on the right-hand edge, and the fishing gear of a boat and the sea wall on the left-hand edge were more difficult. In Figure 3.18 I took a different approach, with the difficult bits being cropped or painted out of the picture altogether. The bit of bowsprit and rigging on the right edge has been painted out for example, as has the rear end of the ship a little higher up. The sea wall in the bottom left-hand corner has also been removed.

Before using the Clone Stamp tool a suitable brush has to be selected, and there is a menu of brushes at the left end of the Options bar, and alternative sets are available via a submenu. The default set of brushes is divided into three main groups, and one of these is the round type that produces well defined lines with "clean" edges. The second group produce simple lines but with fuzzy edges. The third group produce textures and effects. The brushes with blurred edges are good for

Fig.3.18 The retouched "after" version of the image

retouching images, as the fuzzy edges often help blend the newly added material with the original image. A brush with a "hard" edge can be better for fine work where the retouching is being done on a pixel by pixel basis, or something close to it. Filling large areas is quicker and generally more convincing using a large brush, but obviously a small brush is needed for retouching fine detail. It is often a matter of starting with a large brush and moving down to a small one for the final touches. Note that you are not limited to the preset sizes in the brush sets. The Options bar includes a facility for altering the size of the selected brush. You can therefore select any brush of the right type and then alter its size as and when necessary.

In order to paint on the screen using any form of painting tool you hold down the left mouse button while moving the mouse. In the case of the Clone Stamp tool an error message will be produced if you try to use it without first indicating what you wish to clone. You do this by first placing the pointer at the centre of the material you wish to clone and pressing the Alt key. Incidentally, when using any form of brush tool the pointer is actually an outline of the brush. You can therefore see the exact size and shape of the selected brush. When you press the Alt key, the pointer will change to a sort of crosshairs sight. Drag the pointer to the centre of the area that will be retouched, release the left mouse button, and then release the Alt key.

By doing this you are indicating an offset to Photoshop. If you dragged the mouse 70 pixels up and 42 pixels to the left, then it will "paint" using material 70 pixels down and 42 pixels to the right of the brush. You are not restricted to copying to and from the areas indicated when setting the offset. It is possible to paint anywhere on the screen using this offset, but with the proviso that the source must be somewhere on the image. When working near the edge of an image you might find that you are painting with plain white "paint". If this occurs you are trying to clone material from an area outside the image's boundaries, and a new offset is needed.

It is necessary to apply some common sense when using the Clone Stamp tool. Look at the image to find a source that will convincingly cover the object or blemish that is to be removed. In general it is best to use source material that is quite close to the area that will be covered. Material from further afield often looks as though it is suitable, but when you try it there are problems. In most images there are variations in the general level of brightness from one area to another. This can result in the cloned material being noticeably lighter or darker than its immediate surroundings. Like everything else in a photograph, textures and patterns tend to get smaller as they recede into the distance. If a pattern is obviously larger or smaller than its surroundings it will look like a patched area of the photograph. The direction of any lines in a patterned area is another important consideration. There will often be variations and using cloned material that runs at something very close to the correct angle will give the most convincing results.

It is often necessary to copy from more than one source in order to produce convincing results. Even when dealing with background material, copying a large amount from one area to another can produce a fairly obvious duplication. Using more than one source often produces more convincing results anyway. When using the clone tool it is important to bear in mind that it copies from the image as it is when you start each cloning operation. In other words, you can only clone cloned material by starting a new cloning operation.

This could be useful if you need to move something slightly, but it also means that in most situations there is a definite limit on the amount of material that can be cloned in a single operation. The smaller the offset used, the smaller the amount that can be copied without starting to clone the object you are trying to cover. Results are often best with a small offset, but a large offset has the advantage of enabling each operation to clone more material. A compromise therefore has to be sought. If circumstances force the use of a small offset, it is still possible to use a

Fig.3.19 The unprocessed version of the butterfly image

small amount of source material to fill a large area. However, it has to be done in several clone operations rather than one large one.

It is desirable to clone material in as few operations as possible as this makes it quick and easy to produce seamless results. In practice this is not an option if a small offset is used, and copying large areas runs the risk of making the use of cloning too obvious. Due care has to be taken when using numerous small cloning operations to fill a large area. It is easier to end up with odd looking repeating patterns than it is to produce convincing results. Varying the direction and size of the offset helps to avoid or at least disguise any repeating patterns.

Alignment option

When trying to make a small amount of source material go a long way it can be useful to remove the tick in the Alignment checkbox of the Options bar. As already explained, the Clone Stamp tool normally operates using the offset indicated by pressing the Alt key and dragging the pointer. This offset is used wherever you "paint" on the screen. It can be changed at any time by pressing the Alt key and dragging the pointer again, but it can be tedious and time consuming if numerous changes are required.

*Fig.3.20 The hole in the leaf has been retouched in a rather
unconvincing manner at this stage*

Things operate rather differently with the Alignment option switched off. Before using the Clone Stamp tool it is merely necessary to press the Alt key and then left-click on the centre of the area that you wish to copy from. Each time you start painting with the Clone Stamp tool it will start copying from the point that you indicated. In effect, a new offset is indicated and used each time you start using the Clone Stamp tool. Simply press the Alt key and left-click on a different point in order to copy from a different part of the image. Obviously this method can be very useful when it is necessary to copy the same object to various points on the image.

The Opacity control gives normal operation at 100 percent through to an invisibly copy at zero percent. It is sometimes possible to blend the cloned material into the original more convincingly if less than 100 percent opacity is used. With the Alignment option used, it is possible to set a low opacity value and gradually built up the cloned material to the required strength by repeatedly copying it. One slight problem in using less than 100 percent opacity is that it can result in textures in the cloned area of the image being smoothed out. This is almost certain to occur if the cloned material is brought up to the required opacity by copying it from more than one source. There tends to be a sort of averaging process that will certainly alter textures and can lose them altogether.

Fig.3.21 The cloned material has been blended into the surroundings

Healing tool

On trying the Healing tool it will probably seem to work in exactly the same way as the standard Clone Stamp tool. However, rather than just making an exact copy of material it tries to blend it into the surrounding area by adjusting the brightness. Figure 3.19 shows a photograph of a butterfly, and in Figure 3.20 I am in the process of using cloned material to cover the hole in the leaf to the left of the butterfly. The cloned material is from lower down and to the right, and is much lighter than the area around the hole. As things stand, the cloning has simply resulted in the hole being replaced with a light coloured and rather obvious patch! However, on releasing the left mouse button the program made a few adjustments, giving the much improved result of Figure 3.21. The cloned area has been darkened to match the surrounding area.

Spot Healing Brush

This tool represents the quickest and easiest way of removing most unwanted objects or blemishes from a photograph. It is particularly useful with images that have problems with dark spots caused by dust on the camera's sensor. In order to remove something it is just a matter of

Fig.3.22 The fully "cleaned" version of the image

painting over it with this tool. It is selected by right-clicking the button in the toolbar for the Healing Brush, and choosing Spot Healing Brush from the little pop-out menu. Note that many of the buttons in the toolbar have alternative functions that can be selected in this way.

In Figure 3.22 I have painted over the hole in the leaf and various other imperfections in the foliage, and the Spot Healing tool has removed them all very convincingly. Notice how the veins in the leaves run through the relevant healed areas. This tool will try to match each healed area to the surrounding area, maintain lines and patterns as far as possible. The only place in which the Spot Healing tool did not work well was when trying to remove the hole in the leaf just below, and partially covered by the butterfly.

The problem here is that the Spot Healing tool will tend to fill the patched area with a mixture of the green leaf and the orange/brown texture of the butterfly. What is needed though, is just cloned material from the leaf. The Spot Healing tool will often struggle in situations such as this where the area to be patched is next to an abrupt change from one colour and (or) texture to another. In this case I found that the ordinary Clone Stamp tool did the job rather better.

Although it is called the Spot Healing tool, it can handle more than small spots. In Figure 3.23 I have painted over the dinghy on the left-hand

*Fig.3.23 I have painted over the dinghy on the left using the Spot
          Healing tool*

side of the picture, just below the blue fishing boat. On releasing the left
mouse button the dinghy has gone and has been replaced by material
that is based on the surrounding area (Figure 3.24). In fact in Figure
3.24 I have used the Spot Healing Brush to remove the mooring buoy on
the right, the ship on the horizon, and various boats in the background!

Selective processing

Why is it sometimes advantageous to apply processing to only part of
an image? Suppose that you have an image of an object such as a
piece of jewellery, and it is on a rather uninspiring background. You
might decide to paint in a simple graduated background instead of the
original. This type of thing is much used in advertising, where the main
subject is made to look more dynamic and stand out better by replacing
the natural background. It can be used to good effect if you produce
photographs for online auctions or something of this type.

Having to carefully paint around a complex object is very time consuming.
It would clearly be much easier if there was a way of selecting the outline
of the main subject and setting everything within it as a no-go area. It
would then be easy to paint on the background using the brush tools or
using flood fills, as there would be no danger of altering the main subject.

Fig.3.24 The dinghy has been seamlessly removed

Indeed, even if you tried to paint over the main subject it would not be possible to do so.

There are other reasons for using selective processing. For example, sharpening an entire image often works quite well, but it can give some strange looking results with photographs that are a bit "noisy". The noise is most obvious in parts of the image that lack contrast, such as a plain blue area of sky, where the random coloured dots of "noise" do not become partially hidden by the normal textures of the image. There is no point in sharpening these areas since there is no detail to sharpen, and all that will happen is that the "noise" will become about ten times more obvious. Once you have learned to make selections you will soon find plenty of uses for this ability.

The Photoshop selection tools provide various means of selecting areas that can either be used as no-go zones or as the only areas that can be altered. It is only fair to point out that selecting precisely the right part of an image can be quite easy or very difficult depending on the nature of the image. Something that has "hard" edges that contrast well with the background is likely to be easier than something that has "soft" edges with a tendency to blend into the background. Photoshop has tools and functions that help to deal with awkward parts of an image, but there is no guarantee of perfect results every time. With uncooperative images it is necessary to draw at least part of the selection outline by hand.

Fig.3.25 Some useful settings are available from the Options bar

In order to increase the chances of selecting exactly the required areas, Photoshop has several selection tools that operate in different ways. The Marquee tools are the most basic, and the rectangular Marquee tool simply selects the area within a rectangle dragged onto the screen. Although it is a pretty basic method of selection, it is one that you will probably use a fair amount in real-world image processing. The Marquee can be restricted to a square by holding down the Shift key while dragging it onto the screen. There is an elliptical version of the Marquee tool which no doubt has its uses, but it is probably not something that will be used frequently. Note that a circle will be produced if the Shift key is held down while using the Elliptical Marquee tool.

The pointer changes to an arrowhead when it is placed within any marquee, and this indicates that the marquee can be dragged to a different position. The arrowhead is the pointer for the Move tool, and Photoshop is indicating an automatic change to this tool when the pointer is within a marquee. If the Control key is operated while dragging a selection, the contents of the marquee are dragged with it. In effect, a cut and paste operation is performed. Note that dragging the marquee thereafter results in the contents moving with it, and there is no need to hold down the Control after the first time.

Another useful ploy is to operate the Spacebar while dragging a marquee onto the screen. This results in the marquee being moved rather than changed in size. Releasing the Spacebar takes things back to the normal sizing mode. It can be difficult to get it right the first time when using the Marquee tool, but the selection is easily "fine tuned" by switching between the sizing and moving modes via the Spacebar. A further ploy is to hold down the Alt key while dragging a marquee onto the screen. The marquee will then be centred on the starting point. As the marquee is dragged onto the screen, it expands around its starting point.

Making a new selection while an existing selection is present normally results in the original one being deleted. However, it is possible to have multiple selections. Simply hold down the shift key while making a selection and any existing selection or selections will be left on the screen. One slight snag with this method is that it is not possible to use the Shift key to constrain the Marquee to a square or circle, since it is being used to indicate that a multiple selection is required.

Fig.3.26 The inner marquee is a subtraction type

Selection modes

With a Marquee tool selected there are four buttons near the left end of the Options bar and some menus to the right (Figure 3.25). By default the first button (working from left to right) is active, and this sets the selection process to the mode where a new selection replaces any existing ones. Using the next button along sets the mode where multiple selections are possible. Note that in the multiple mode any overlapping selections are merged into a single selection. If necessary, quite complex shapes can be built up in this way.

The third button puts the Marquee tool into Subtraction mode, which enables a "hole" or "knockout" to be placed within an existing selection. It can also be used to nibble pieces from the edge of the exiting selection. In Figure 3.26 I first used the Elliptical Marquee tool to place a large ellipse around the flower, and then using the Subtraction mode a smaller ellipse was placed around the middle of the flower. The Delete key was then operated so that the selected area was erased, which is only the area between the two ellipses (Figure 3.27). This clearly shows how the area within the smaller ellipse has been removed from the selection, since this part of the initial selection has not been erased.

The final button is the Intersect with Selection button. Normally two overlapping selections are merged to make one large selection. In the

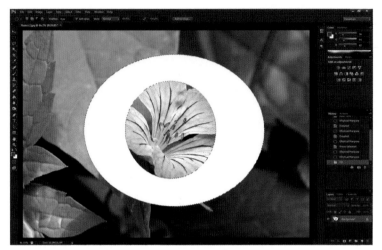

Fig.3.27 The subtracted area has not been deleted

Intersect mode things operate in the opposite manner, with only the overlapping sections being used in the combined selection. This method can be used to produce selections having shapes that are not otherwise possible using the basic Marquee tools.

Mode

Three options are available from the Style menu on the Options bar. By default the Normal style is selected, and the Marquee tools then work in the standard fashion described previously. As one would expect, using the Fixed Ratio mode results in rectangular and elliptical selections having a fixed aspect ratio. This is rather like holding down the Shift key to force a square or circular selection, but other aspect ratios are possible.

The Width and Height textboxes just to the right of the menu become active when this mode is selected. The default aspect ratio is 1 to 1, but any desired ratio can be entered in the textboxes. The third option is for a marquee of a fixed size, and the two textboxes are again active when this option is selected. They are used to set the width and height of the marquee in pixels. In this mode the marquee is produced by left-clicking the mouse. Dragging the marquee obviously has no effect on its size, but instead moves it around the screen. Consequently, there is no need to hold down the Spacebar in order to move the marquee.

Once in position it can be moved in the normal way, and multiple selections are still possible. In Figure 3.28 a series of circular selections were added to produce the desired shape. Then the Inverse option was chosen from the Select menu so that the area within the selection was deselected, and everything else became the new selection. The selection was then erased by pressing the Delete key.

Do not press the Delete key in order to clear marquees from the screen. As we have already seen, this will delete the selected material, leaving the marquee in place. One or more marquees can be deselected by left-clicking anywhere on the image provided Normal mode is selected and the New Selection button is active. This effectively replaces the current selection with a new one having zero pixels. In the New Selection and Intersect modes it is possible to remove the current selection or selections by left-clicking within one of the selections. Another method is to right-click on a selection and select Deselect from the popup menu. Note that this clears away all the selections if there is more than one, and not just the selection that was right-clicked. The Deselect option is also available from the Select menu on the menu bar (Select-Deselect).

Lasso tool

The Marquee tools are adequate for many selection tasks, but they make heavy work of selecting complex shapes. It can be done, but a lot of merging and nibbling is needed to get things right. The Lasso tool is better for selecting awkward shapes since it enables you to draw around the required area. Although it is easy to use in theory, in practice it is difficult to use the Lasso tool with adequate accuracy. Even an experienced and skilled user is unlikely to get it right first time. At first it is often a struggle to get anything approximating to the required selection.

A digitising tablet and a stylus is certainly much better than a mouse for this type of thing, and an inexpensive digitising tablet is certainly a worthwhile investment for anyone who uses Photoshop more than occasionally. The merge and subtraction methods work using the Lasso tool, so it is possible to "fine tune" the selection if you do not get it right first time. It is easier to get good accuracy using a zoomed view, so make good use of the pan and zoom facilities when making fine adjustments. Most people find that reducing the sensitivity of the mouse or tablet makes it easier to obtain good accuracy. By reducing sensitivity I mean that the pointing device should be set so that more physical movement is required for a given amount of movement on the screen.

Fig.3.28 This selection is comprised of several circles

To use the Lasso tool you simply drag a line around the area that you wish to select. There is no need to accurately match the start and finish points of the line. Photoshop will automatically connect the start and finish points. On the other hand, leaving a large gap is unlikely to give adequate accuracy. With practice and the inevitable fine adjustments to the marquee, it will usually be possible to obtain the desired result.

Polygonal Lasso tool

There are two alternative versions of the Lasso tool available, and the first of them is the Polygonal Lasso tool. This is used to draw irregular polygons, and on the face of it the regular Lasso tool is the more useful. The polygonal version draws straight lines between points drawn on the screen, which means that true curves cannot be produced. There is no such limitation with the normal Lasso tool, where freehand drawing can be used to produce any shape, curved or otherwise.

However, as already explained, accurate drawing using the normal Lasso tool is very difficult. Even after you have gained some experience it can be very difficult to get really good accuracy without resorting to a great deal of "fine tuning". Drawing complex shapes by picking points on the outline is very much easier. Although it is not possible to draw true curves,

Fig.3.29 The Magnetic Lasso tool has done a good job here

a good approximation can be produced using several short lines.   In practice, selections made using Polygonal Lasso tool are often sufficiently accurate without the need for fine adjustments, which is rarely if ever true when using the normal Lasso tool.

Magnetic Lasso tool

This is a sort of semiautomatic version of the standard Lasso tool. As already pointed out, getting accurate results using the normal Lasso tool is quite tricky. Photoshop will faithfully reproduce every little error in your rendering of the outline, and some editing will usually be required once the outline has been completed. The Magnetic Lasso tool makes life much easier by looking for an outline to follow rather than simply following the exact path of the pointer. How well or otherwise this works depends on how well an objects outline is defined. It should work very well if there is plenty of contrast in shade or colour. If there is no outline to follow, the Magnetic Lasso is not the tool for the job. It is probably not the best tool for the job if there is only an indistinct or intermittent outline to follow.

The flower in the test photograph stands out well from the background, and it did quite a good job of separating the flower from the background (Figure 3.29).   Here I have inverted the selection and erased the background so it is easy to see exactly what was selected. It is not quite perfect, but a minimal amount of work would be needed in order to tidy things up.

There are some parameters in the Options bar that enable the Magnetic Lasso tool to be optimised for a given situation. The Width (detection width) setting controls how close the pointer has to be to an edge for the Magnetic Lasso tool to latch onto it. The larger this figure the less accurately you have to follow the outline. Do not be tempted to use a large figure for this setting though. The line might tend to jump off its intended path and onto another outline, particularly if the pointer is allowed to stray well away from the correct path. The Width setting is in pixels incidentally.

The Contrast figure determines the difference in brightness value required for an outline to be recognised. Using a low value enables the outline to be followed even when there is relatively little contrast between the object and the background. Unfortunately, it also increases the likelihood of the line jumping over to a different outline or jumping to any small areas of slight contrast. A small Contrast value normally has to be accompanied by a small Width value and careful drawing of the selection outline. This tool works best with well defined objects and a reasonably high Contrast value.

The Frequency setting controls the number of anchor points that will be added as the outline is drawn. These anchor points are shown as tiny squares on the line while it is being drawn. The higher the number, the more anchor points that are used and the more accurately intricate outlines can be tracked. A high value gives better accuracy with this type of thing, but note that the maximum permissible value is 100. On the down side, a high value might have a tendency to produce rough edges, particularly when used with a low Contrast value.

Using the Magic Lasso tool is again very straightforward. Drag the line making sure that the pointer is kept quite close to the outline you are trying to follow. Release the left mouse button when the pointer is back at the starting point. Alternatively, double click the mouse with the pointer close to the starting point. Photoshop will then draw a line from between the final and starting points, tracking what it considers to be the correct path.

If things go badly wrong, operate the Escape key to completely remove the line so that you can start from scratch. The last anchor point added can be removed by operating the delete key, and this key can be operated repeatedly to remove further anchor points back down the line. Keep

Fig.3.30 Deleting the selection shows that it contains numerous small islands

the pointer still while deleting anchor points so that no new ones are added while you are trying to remove some of the existing points. This tool often gives better results with the pointer kept just to one side of the required path rather than trying to track the pointer right over the path.

Magic Wand tool

With the Magic Wand tool there is no need to draw around the object you wish to select. You just left-click at a suitable point on the image and Photoshop automatically selects the right area. Of course, in reality it is not quite as simple as that, and Photoshop might not get it right. The Magic Wand tool tries to find an outline based on the colour values of the pixels. If there is good colour contrast between the object you are trying to select and the background it is likely that the Magic Wand tool will do a good job. Results are less sure if the object blends into the background at some points.

With the Magic Wand tool it is not usually a matter of just left-clicking once on the image and the required selection is made. In the real world it is usually necessary to use the Add to Selection mode and a number

Fig.3.31 The selection has been cleaned and then blurred

of mouse clicks in order to build up the required selection. This was the method used with the butterfly picture in Figure 3.30, where it is the greenery in the background rather than the butterfly that has been selected. Operating the Delete key then produced the result of Figure 3.30, where it is clear that the butterfly is intact, but numerous little islands in the selection have been left. These are caused by tiny blemishes on the leaves that are very different in tone and colour to the surrounding area. This type of thing can be cleaned up quite quickly using the Marquee or Lasso tool in the Add to Selection mode. In Figure 3.31 I have cleaned up the selection, inverted it, and use the Average Blur filter to produce a plain green background. Using the Paint Bucket tool the background could be set at any desired colour, or a fancy background could be added using the Gradient tool.

With the poppy picture of Figure 3.32 I took the opposite approach to the butterfly example. The outline of the poppy has relatively little colour variation, whereas the background is much more varied. It was easy to select areas around the periphery of the poppy, and a Marquee tool was then used to add everything within this selection. This produced quite an accurate selection that was free from "islands". In Figure 3.33 I have inverted the selection and then blurred the background using the

Fig.3.32 Here it is easier to select the poppy than the background

Gaussian Blur filter (Filter-Blur-Gaussian Blur) to give the picture a "dreamy" quality.

Fig.3.33 The selection has been inverted and then blurred

Settings

There are a few Magic Wand settings available from the Options bar. The tolerance setting is important, and it is unlikely that good results will be obtained unless this is adjusted to suit each task. It controls the amount of colour contrast that is needed for Photoshop to perceive the change as an edge. If it is set too low there will be very little selected, but practically everything will be included if it is set too high. A little trial and error will probably be needed in order to find the best value for a given image.

Contiguous

By default the Contiguous checkbox is ticked, which means that a continuous path of pixels is sought by the program, which tries to find an outline. It will also find any "islands" within the outline and automatically subtract them from the selection. The Magic Wand tool simply selects any pixels of colours within its tolerance setting when this checkbox is not ticked. In other words, it tries to find any pixels of the right colour range, anywhere on the image, and it does not try to find outlines.

Anti-aliased

The Anti-aliased checkbox is also ticked by default. This is also available and used by default with the Lasso tools. Anti-aliasing smoothes the edges of the selection or selections, which often gives better results than having it faithfully follow every nook and cranny in an outline. On the other hand, anti-aliasing will probably give less satisfactory results if the required selection genuinely has rough edges. The smoothing will cause parts of the required area to be omitted and (or) material outside the required area to be included. With an area that has a smooth and well defined outline it is unlikely to make much difference one way or the other. Once again, it is a matter of experimenting to find the mode that gives the best results.

Select menu

Do not overlook the facilities available from the Select menu. A similar but different menu is also available by right-clicking within a selection. A Feather option is available when some selection tools are selected, and it also appears in the Options bar when appropriate. It is available directly from the right-click menu, but with the Select menu it is in the Modify submenu (Select-Modify-Feather). It is primarily intended for use with cut/copy and paste operations. There can be problems with objects

Fig.3.34 A mask has been painted over the butterfly

that are pasted into an image having a two dimensional cardboard cut-out appearance.

Feathering offers one approach to integrating a pasted object into an image without getting the cardboard cut-out effect. It gives a blurred edge that blends into the new image more realistically, and the width of the feathering (in pixels) can be specified on the Options bar prior to selection. A small dialogue box appears when Feathering is chosen from a menu, and this is used to specify a value for the pixel width. This method can be used to add feathering to an existing selection.

There are four other options available in the Modify submenu. The Border option produces a small dialogue box that requests a pixel value to be entered. Instead of selecting the area within an outline, a band of pixels centred on the outline is selected. The value entered controls the width of the band. The Smooth option does precisely that, and it will smooth out jagged edges in the marquee. The Expand and Contract options simply enlarge or shrink the selection by the specified number of pixels.

One application of the last two options is to take slightly more of an image than is really required for a copy and paste operation. The pasted background is then painted over using the existing background of the destination image. This is not a quick way of doing things, but it ensures that all the required source material is copied with no little bits missing, and the pasted image should integrate quite well with the rest of the

*Fig.3.35 Back in normal operation the mask is effectively an inverse
          selection*

destination image. You may find that some selection methods tend to
outline slightly too much or too little material. The Expand and Contract
options provide quick and easy solutions to these problems.

The Grow option in the main Select menu should not be confused with
the Expand option in the Modify submenu. Grow does not expand the
border of the selection by a certain number of pixels. Instead, it looks for
pixels of a similar colour around the border, and the selection then grows
into these. The point of this is to add minor omissions from the edge of
selection without introducing extraneous material, which is a problem
that is likely to occur with the Expand option.

As we have already seen, the Inverse option simply deselects everything
that is currently selected, and selects everything that was not previously
selected. It is often easier to select the background and then use the
Inverse option to select the main subject matter, rather than taking the
more direct route of trying to select the main subject.

Quick Mask mode

Perhaps the obvious way of making a selection is to use a brush tool
and then use it to paint over the parts of the image that you wish to
select. There is no feature of this type available in Photoshop, but there

Fig.3.36 The background has been delected and replaced

is one that effectively provides this facility. The second button from the bottom in the Toolbar provides two modes of operation, which are the Standard and Quick Mask modes. You can also toggle between the two using the Q key of the keyboard. The Standard mode is used by default, but switching to the Quick Mask mode enables a mask to be painted onto the screen. Figure 3.34 is a photograph of a holy blue butterfly laying eggs on an ivy plant, and I have used the ordinary Brush tool to paint over the butterfly. However, you can use any of the painting and drawing tools to create a mask, and the Eraser tool can be used to remove pieces of the mask.

With something fairly intricate such as this it is necessary to zoom in and use a small brush when painting over finer parts and when defining edges, but a large brush can then be used to quickly fill the interior. It will often be quite time consuming when using this method, but you set your own level of accuracy. A pixel perfect but time consuming mask can be made, a "rough and ready" one can be quickly laid down, or you can settle for anything between these two extremes.

Fig.3.37 The Quick Selection tool has worked reasonably well here

Having completed the mask, go back to the standard mask and the painted area becomes a mask (Figure 3.35). What you really have is an ordinary selection, but with everything but the masked area selected. Use the Inverse command (Select-Inverse) to swap things around so that the mask becomes the selection. In this case I left the mask as such, used the Delete key to remove everything but the butterfly, and added a yellow background using the Paint Bucket tool (Figure 3.36). I did not attempt a pixel-perfect mask, but even so it has produced quite accurate results.

Quick Selection tool

The Quick Selection Tool (beneath the Magic Wand tool) is a bit like an "intelligent" version of the Quick Mask mode, but it produces a selection not a mask, and it removes the need to carefully paint up to borders. Instead you just click or drag the brush within the area you wish to select, and the border will be found automatically. As with any automatic selection system, it works better with some things than it does with others.

In Figure 3.37 it took only a few seconds to find the outline of the butterfly and delete the back ground, but some further work is required. Some of

Fig.3.38 The Quick Selection tool has worked very accurately here

the background has been included on the left-hand side, and the butterfly's antennae have been omitted. This tool works best with fairly large areas, and it was difficult to include the antennae even when using a very small brush size. The Magic Wand tool proved to be much better for this task. The Quick Selection worked much better at selecting the blackbird in Figure 3.38, and the original selection required a minimum of "fine tuning". In Figure 3.39 the selection has been inverted and the background was then blurred using the Gaussian Blur filter.

The Options bar has three buttons that give New Selection, Add to Selection, and Subtract from Selection modes. There is also an Auto Enhance option that follows outlines better, with fewer rough edges on the one hand, but without taking an over simplistic approach. Results are usually much better when using this option, but it might cause the Quick Selection tool to operate quite slowly.

Patch tool

The Patch tool is similar to the Healing Brush tool, and it is grouped with the healing tools on the Toolbar, but it works with selections rather than in brush fashion. The pointer effectively becomes the Lasso tool when this Patch tool is selected, and selections are made using the normal

Fig.3.39 The selection has been inverted and the background has been blurred

Lasso tool facilities and techniques. The Options bar has two radio buttons that enable the selection to be used as the source or the destination. When it is used as the source you can drag the selection to a different part of the image, and it will then be copied to that location. The original selection stays in place, so it is a copying action and not a move type that is obtained.

In Figure 3.40 I have selected the area around the dinghy near the middle of the picture, and its reflection in the sea. Copy and move operations are unlikely to be convincing unless any reflections or shadows are selected together with the main subject. I first copied the dinghy slightly to the left of the original selection, and then I dragged it again, this time to the right, to produce a further copy (Figure 3.41). Each time a copy is made using the Patch tool there will be a short delay while the copy is merged into the background.

In this example the copy on the left is in a lighter part of the picture, and the boat has been made a bit lighter to match this. The copy on the right

Fig.3.40 *The area around the dinghy has been selected*

is in a darker part of the picture, and the dinghy has therefore been made slightly darker. The copies fit in quite well with the background, and the modified picture is quite good as it stands. However, it could be

Fig.3.41 *Two copies of the dinghy have been added*

Fig.3.42 Here the dinghy has been erased and automatically replaced by material based on the surrounding area

improved by some manual editing in two or three places, which is normally the case with this type of thing.

When the Destination mode is selected, the Patch tool lives up to its name and the selected area will be patched with material cloned from elsewhere on the image. As before, the selection is dragged to a new position on the image, and material from that area will be used as the basis of the patch. The area originally selected shows the material that will be used as the patch, making it easier to find source material that is likely to give good results. In Figure 3.42 I have used the same selection as before, but with the Destination mode so that the dinghy is expunged from the image. The end result is reasonably convincing, especial when the large size of the patch is taken into account. As before though, a bit of manual editing would probably produce a worthwhile improvement.

Move

The Patch tool can be used to patch images and copy objects, but it cannot be used to move them. There is a separate tool for doing this in the form of the Content Aware Move tool, which is grouped with the Patch tool and the other cloning tools. It operates in a similar fashion to the Patch tool. First you select the material to be moved, and then drag it to the new location. In Figure 3.43 I have dragged the selection to the

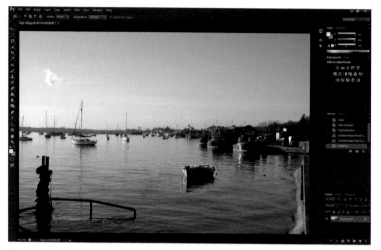

Fig.3.43 In this example the dinghy has been moved to the right

right, and the dinghy has duly been relocated. The blank area left by the change has been automatically filled to match the surrounding background.

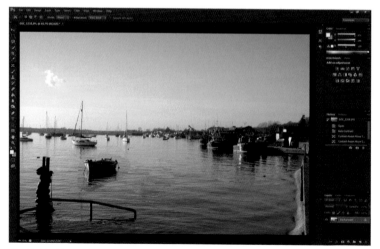

Fig.3.44 Here the Very Strict option had to be used

Fig.3.45 Lightening the selection has given better results

The Adaption menu offers five levels of adaption from Very Loose to Very Strict, with Medium being used by default. Although the Very Strict option is the one that should work best, it is possible that a lower setting will give better results with some images. In the example of Figure 3.43 I found that the default Medium setting gave the best results. In the example of Figure 3.44 I moved the dinghy slightly the other way, and it required the Very Strict setting to get the change to look even semi-convincing. The dingy and the area of sea selected with it are noticeably darker that the part of the image they have been moved to. With this type of thing it pays to bear in mind that the moved material is a selection, and that the full range of brightness, contrast, and colour controls can be applied to it without altering the rest of the image. In Figure 3.45 I have lightened the selection very slightly, which has given a much more plausible end result.

There is a Content Aware option available from the Options bar when using the Patch tool. The Adaption menu becomes available when this mode is selected, but the Source and Destination options disappear. Consequently, it can still be used for removing objects and patching the gap that is left behind, but the ability to copy objects to another part of the image is lost.

*Fig.3.46 The blackbird has been pasted onto the dandelion picture,
but it has been placed on a new layer*

Layers

A selection can be copied from one image and pasted into another, and I have done this in the jokey example of Figure 3.46. First the selection in Figure 3.38 was copied using the normal Copy option in the Edit menu. Then the image of the dandelion and hoverfly was loaded into Photoshop, and the Paste option in the Edit menu was used to add the blackbird selection to this image. The Move tool was then used to shift the blackbird into position. It then becomes clear that the reason for the blackbird looking so happy is that she has spotted a juicy meal!

Paste operations can be a bit confusing for newcomers to Photoshop as the pasted material is automatically placed onto a new layer. New layers are generated by some other facilities of Photoshop. For example, each piece of text that is added using the Text tool is automatically placed onto its own layer. Without realising it, you can soon have quite a large number of layers that Photoshop has generated. As a consequence of this, you find that most of the image cannot be edited, or so it appears anyway.

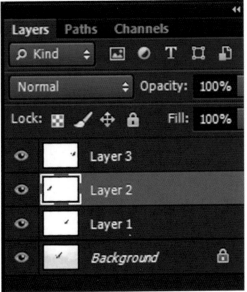

Fig.3.47 The Layers panel

The point of using one layer per element in the image is that it makes it easy to edit each element separately. For example, text or pasted material can be moved by selecting the correct layer and then dragging it using the Move tool. There is no need to bother about selecting the material that must be moved, since there is nothing else on that layer. Move the entire layer and you move the required elements in the image. There is no need to heal gaps left when the material is moved, because it does not leave any.

Think of layers in terms of each one being on a separate piece of transparent film, with the pieces of film laid one on top of the other. Material on a piece of film near the top of the pile will obscure some of the material on lower layers. If the layer is moved to one side, the obscured material can be seen, but a different part of the image is obscured on the lower layers. Hence objects can be moved around without the need to fill in any gaps left by the changes.

Automatically generated layers can give beginners problems because the new layer becomes the current one, and it is not possible to edit anything on another layer. Attempts to do so either have no effect or produce error messages. Normally it is only possible to edit the current layer. The Layers panel has a list of all the layers in the image, and initially there is just one that is called Background. Any layers that are added by text or paste operations are added above any existing layers, and they are called Layer 1, Layer 2, Layer 3, and so on. The Layers panel can be seen in in Figure 3.47. The position of a layer in the list is the same as its position in the image. For example, Layer 2 is on top of

Fig.3.48 This picture will be given the soft focus treatment

Layer 1 and the Background layer, and anything on Layer 2 therefore covers these lower layers. Similarly, anything on Layer 3 would obstruct the view of Layer 2 and the lower layers. Apart from the Background layer, it is possible to move a layer to a new position in the list and the image by dragging its name to a new position in the list.

Transparency

A layer does not have to be opaque, and the opacity can be altered by left clicking its entry in the list to make it the current one, and typing an opacity value in the text box near the top right-hand corner of the Layers panel. The control range runs from zero percent (completely transparent) to one hundred percent (totally opaque). Image processing that makes use of layers is often dependent on one

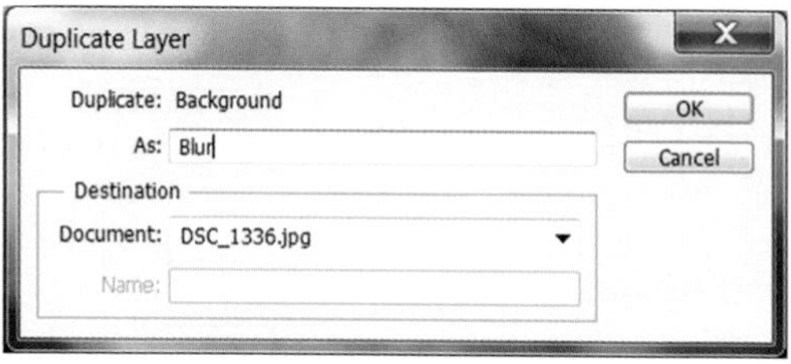

Fig.3.49 The background layer is duplicated

Fig.3.50 The blurred duplicate layer

or more layers being semi-transparent. A soft focus effect is a good example of this. The Gaussian Blur filter is useful for adding a soft focus effect, but it is important to realise that a soft focus effect is not the same as simply blurring the image slightly. Simply adding some Gaussian Blur filtering produces a blurred image and not a soft focus effect. A soft focus effect is produced by having a mixture of a sharp image and one that is very blurred.

Soft focus

A soft focus effect can be produced by having a sharp background image with a blurred image on Layer 1. Low opacity in the blurred image gives a mild soft focus effect, but the effect gets stronger if the opacity is increased. In Figure 3.48 a sharp background image has been loaded. The next step is to right-click the Background layer's entry in the Layers panel, and then the Duplicate Layer is selected from the pop-up menu. This produces the pop-up window of Figure 3.49. Here a name for the new layer is entered into the textbox, and the OK button is operated to go ahead and produce the new layer. The new layer will be automatically set as the current one, so the blurring can be added by selecting the required filtering from the Filter menu. I used Gaussian Blurring, as most of the other types are not really suitable for this application.

Fig.3.51 The two layers have been combined

Using too little blur filtering is a common error when adding a soft focus effect. If any detail is still visible in the blurred image, mixing it with the sharp image produces a blurred image rather than a soft focus effect. It is preferable to have the broad areas of colour retained from the original image, but all detail must be lost in the blurring. Do not take the filtering so far that a virtually plain image is produced. Adding a totally blurred image with a sharp one tends to produce a large loss of contrast with a relatively weak soft focus effect. Something like the degree of filtering shown in Figure 3.50 should give good results. Various Opacity values are then tried until the desired effect is obtained (Figure 3.51).

The effect can often be improved by slightly increasing the contrast and colour saturation or vibrance, and adding a little sharpening (Figure 3.52). This counteracts the drop in contrast that the soft-focus effect produces, but does not significantly reduce the effect. One way to do this is to first choose the Flatten Image or Merge Visible option from the Layers menu. This merges everything into the Background layer, which can then be processed normally. The image can then be saved in a normal image format such as JPEG or TIFF. Of course, the layer information is lost once the image has been merged into one layer and saved in a standard image format. If you wish to retain layer information it is essential to save the image in Adobe's PSD format prior to merging the layers.

Fig.3.52 The finished version of the soft focus cat

Graduated filter

Layers and the opacity control are useful for producing effects similar to those obtained by using graduated filters over the camera's lens. For this example a graduated tobacco filter will be simulated. These are

Fig.3.53 The non-filtered version of the boat image

often used to give an orange/brown tint to the sky while leaving the foreground unaltered. I used the image of Figure 3.53 as the base image, and I have already added a blank layer by selecting New and then Layer from the Layer menu.

The next step is to add the graduated colour, which must go from orange/brown at the top of the frame to transparent at the bottom. This is easily achieved using the Gradient tool from the toolbar. This is

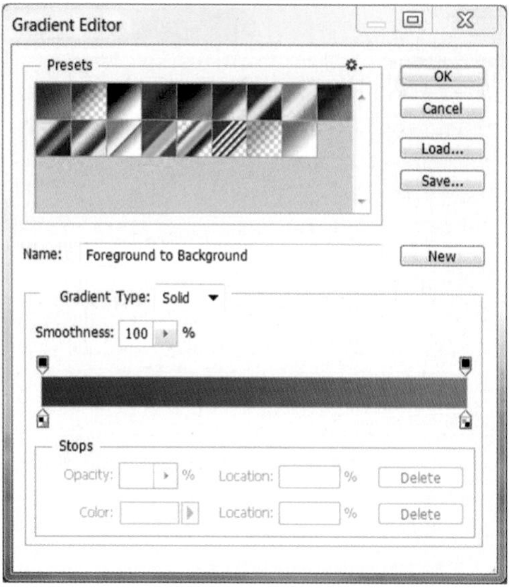

Fig.3.54 The Gradient Editor

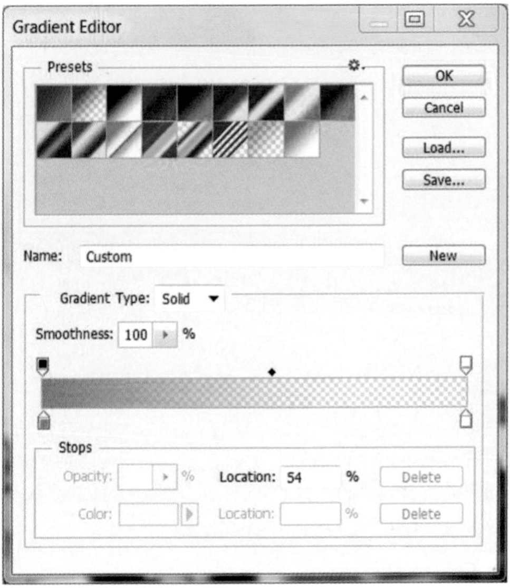

Fig.3.55 The edited gradient

grouped with the Paint Bucket tool. The default colour gradient will be shown near the left end of the Options bar when this tool is selected, but the gradient will have to be edited to suit this application. Left or right clicking the little colour gradient in the Options bar produces the pop-up window of Figure 3.54. There are several preset gradients in the upper part of this window, and for our purposes it is the one that goes from any colour to transparent that is needed as an easy starting point. A chequered pattern in a little square is used to indicate transparency is provided rather than a colour. Simply left-click the required preset colour graduation to select it.

The next step is to change the colour to the required tobacco filter colour. First left click on the little marker at the bottom left-hand corner of the gradient bar in the lower part of the window. Then Right or left-click on the little coloured rectangle near the bottom left-hand corner of the window, which will launch the colour mixer window. There are various ways of setting the required colour, but the easiest is to adjust the big slider control to produce a suitable range of colours in the main panel. Then left-click a colour in the main panel to select it, and click the OK button to close the window. It is advisable to repeat this process for the bottom right-hand marker on the graduation bar, but this time check that the selected colour is pure white with the Red, Green and Blue values all set at 255. This should give something like Figure 3.55, giving the required orange/brown to transparent gradient. Left-click the OK button when back at the Gradient Editor, and you are then ready to add the colour gradient.

Fig.3.56 The graduated filtering has been applied to the image

This is done by dragging a line onto the screen, and the gradient is controlled by the position, length, and direction of the line. In this case we need the colour at the top of the picture and transparency at the bottom, and this is achieved using a vertical line, starting at the top. Holding down the Shift key while dragging the line will keep it perfectly vertical. A short line gives a rapid transition from colour to transparency, and a long line gives a gradual change. A short line half way up the screen therefore gives a rapid transition at that point, while a line from the top of the picture to the bottom gives the most gradual transition. It is really just a matter of using trial and error to find the best effect, using the Undo function to remove the existing gradient before trying another one. Start with the opacity control at about fifty percent, and then adjust it for the best effect once a suitable gradient has been found. Figure 3.56 shows the filter effect that I finally settled for.

A neutral density (ND) graduated filter effect can be obtained using exactly the same method just described, but with black or a neutral grey being selected instead of a colour. Neutral density filters are often used to darken skies that are much brighter than the land in the foreground. Most of the sky in the photograph of Figure 3.57 is very bright, and when viewed on a monitor it is a bit hard on the viewer's eyes. In Figure 3.58 the upper part of the picture has been darkened using a graduated neutral filter effect, and this has tamed the over bright sky.

Fig.3.57 The original version of the churchyard image

Adjustment layers

An adjustment layer is a special type of layer that contains adjustment details for the image on a lower layer. A set of adjustments is all that an adjustment layer can contain, and you cannot paint or draw on this type of layer. An adjustment layer can be added by selecting New Adjustment Layer from the Layer menu, and then the required type of adjustment from the submenu (Figure 3.59). The options available here are essentially the same as the ones in the Adjustments submenu. There is also a button at the bottom of the Layers palette that enables a new adjustment layer to be produced. Either way, the small dialogue box of Figure 3.60 will appear. A few parameters can be changed here, but for most purposes the default settings will suffice.

Having created the layer, the appropriate control dialogue box will appear, which is the Photo Filter type in the example of Figure 3.61. Notice also, that the new layer is now included in the Layers palette near the bottom right-hand corner of the screen. Adjustments to the controls will be applied to the image in the normal way, and in Figure 3.61 a deep blue filter has been used.

Fig.3.58 The filtering has darkened the upper part of the sky

If you change your mind and wish to revert to the original version of the image it is just a matter of deleting the adjustment layer. The adjustment layer can be deleted by left-clicking its entry in the Layers panel to make it the current layer and then selecting Delete and Layer from the Layer menu (Layer-Delete-Layer). Alternatively, drag its entry in the Layers palette to the trashcan icon in the bottom left-hand corner of the palette. The image can be merged into a single layer if you wish to make the changes permanent. Select Flatten from the Layers menu. The changes will be retained but the adjustment layer will be deleted. Note that the image will automatically be flattened if it is saved in a format that does not support adjustment layers, such as Jpeg. Save the image in Photoshop's PSD format if you wish to retain adjustment layers.

More than one type of control can be implemented by adjustment layers, but a different layer must be used for each type of control. You can use one for adjusting colour balance and another for setting the brightness and contrast, for example. The Layers palette provides an Opacity setting near the top right-hand corner (Figure 3.47). This may seem to have no relevance to some adjustment layers, but it permits the changes provided by the layer to be reduced. For example, if the layer provides increased contrast, reducing the opacity setting reduces the boost in contrast. At

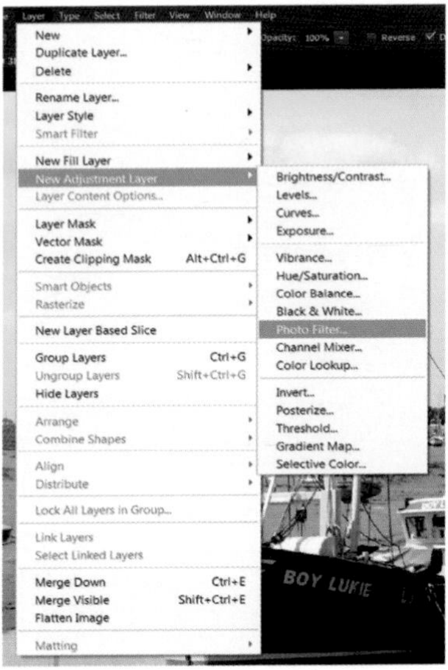

Fig.3.59 Adjustment layer submenu

zero percent opacity the changes are removed completely.

At first sight there may seem to be no point in using adjustment layers. However, an important point to bear in mind is that when making a normal adjustment it is not possible to go back and alter it. In fact you can do so after a fashion via the History panel, but only by deleting other changes as well as the one you wish to alter. You can also call up the type of adjustment in question and use it a second time, but this will not necessarily permit the changes you wish to make. If the original adjustment resulted in detail being clipped for example, subsequent changes to the levels will not recover that detail. Adjustment layers are more versatile and give greater freedom to change your mind, but they also tend to complicate matters. When making a few basic changes it is unlikely that there will be any point in using adjustment layers, and adjustment layers of the required types might not be available anyway. Only a limited range of editing can be performed via this method.

Selective tools

Using the selection tools to restrict what would otherwise be global processing was covered earlier in this chapter, but some of the brush style tools in the toolbar provide a simple alternative to some types of selective processing. The Dodge, Burn, and Sponge tools for instance, respectively enable the processed parts of the image to be lightened, darkened, or have reduced saturation. There are also Blur, Sharpen, and Smudge tools, the latter giving an effect that is a bit like using your finger to rub a painting when the paint is still wet. The History Brush takes the processed parts of the image back to a selected position in the History panel. This is used when you wish to apply processing to most of an image but not quite all of it. Using the History Brush you can trim back the processing from the areas where it is not required.

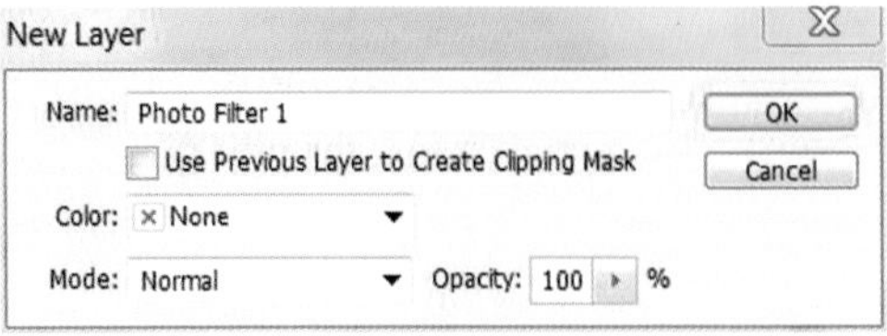

It will probably require a certain amount of practice before you become proficient with these brush tools, but in some circumstances they will provide the desired result much

New Layer

Name: Photo Filter 1

☐ Use Previous Layer to Create Clipping Mask

Color: ✕ None ▼

Mode: Normal ▼ Opacity: 100 ▸ %

OK

Cancel

Fig.3.60 The New dialogue box

more quickly and easily than using the marquee selection tools. The initial brush size will have to be chosen carefully, and as is often the case with brush tools, a smaller size will probably be needed in order to do some "fine tuning". Other parameters might have to be adjusted in order to obtain the desired effect.

Actions

You may find that you perform exactly the same sequence of adjustments very frequently. Most of the illustrations in this book for example, have to be set for a size of 10 centimetres wide at 300 dots per inch, and then converted from RGB colour mode to the CMYK type. It would clearly save a great deal of time if even a short sequence of adjustments such as this could be recorded and then applied to an image by operating a function key. This is possible via the Actions panel. If it is not already

Fig.3.61 The adjustment layer has added blue filtering

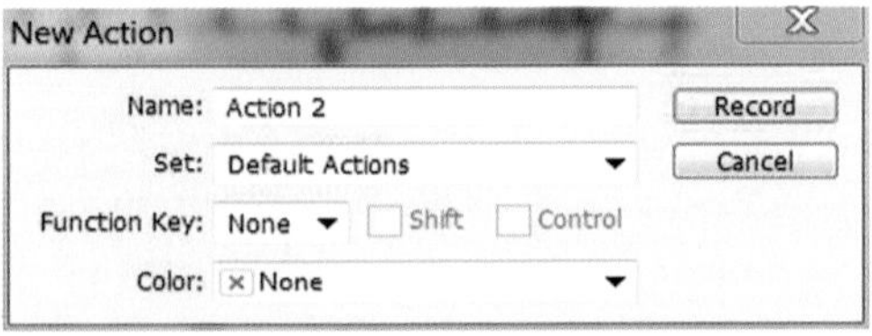

Fig.3.62 The New Action dialogue box

active it can be switched on by selecting Actions from the Window menu (Window-Actions).

In order to record a new set of adjustments it is necessary to have a suitable image loaded into Photoshop. In addition to giving Photoshop something to work with while the actions are being recorded, it also enables the user to check that everything is proceeding according to plan and that no errors have been made. Loading an image is a recordable action, so you could start by loading an image, but I am not sure if there is any practical application of always loading the same image and performing the same actions on it.

There are a series of small control buttons along the bottom of the Actions panel, and the first step in recording a series of adjustments is to operate the Create New Action button, which is the second one from the right end. This brings up the small dialogue box of Figure 3.62, where a name for the new action can be entered into the upper textbox. You can simply settle for the default name, but as with anything like this it is better to choose a meaningful name that will make it easy to find the required set of adjustments.

Next use the Function Key drop-down menu to select the function key that will trigger the set of adjustments. Optionally, the Shift or Control checkbox can be ticked, and the actions will then be triggered by holding down the selected key and operating the chosen function key. Note that the recorded actions do not have to be initiated from the keyboard. Selecting an action from the list and then operating the Play Selection button (the fourth button from the left) provides an alternative method. For this reason it is not essential to select a key or keys to start a set of actions, but the keyboard approach is probably the better one.

It is then a matter of operating the Record button, which will close the dialogue box, and going through the required set of adjustments. Operate the Stop Recording button when you have completed the full sequence of actions. This button is the one at the left end of the row. In order to use the recorded action it is just a matter of selecting the appropriate key or keys, or playing it via the appropriate button on the Actions panel. You can delete any unwanted action by dragging its entry in the list to the bin button, which is the one at the right end of the row.

Adobe
Camera RAW

RAW facts

The Adobe Camera RAW add-on is something that anyone who uses Photoshop in conjunction with a suitable camera should have installed. It is a form of photo editor, but it is used prior to loading a RAW file into Photoshop. A RAW file is basically just the raw data from the camera's sensor. It will not have undergone any form of processing in the camera such as changes to the white balance. RAW files are preferred by photographers who require the highest possible picture quality, because RAW files are not compressed, and do not have the loss in quality associated with compressed image formats such as the ever popular JPEG type.

One of the main attractions of RAW files is that problems with something like a totally inappropriate white balance setting will not affect a RAW file. A mistake of this type will be applied to images that the camera saves in the JPEG format, and correcting the error convincingly by editing a JPEG image in Photoshop could be difficult. In fact there is no guarantee that it can be done without some loss of image quality. A RAW file is the unprocessed data from the camera's sensor, and it is not subjected to any white balance or other corrections. Anything of this type is applied later using an image editor. A RAW file will not necessarily produce significantly better results than a JPEG type that is a bit "wide of the mark", but in many cases it will do so.

One drawback of RAW files is that they are relatively large. One of my cameras produces RAW files that are about 25 megabytes per file. The highest quality JPEG files it produces are around 6 to 7 megabytes per file. Many of the more upmarket cameras can save RAW files and JPEG versions, giving the convenience of one and the quality of the other. Of course, this results in even larger amounts of data being placed on the memory card each time a photograph is taken, but it is a method that has a lot of followers despite this.

Another problem with RAW files is they are not a standard format like JPEG, TIFF, and other normal image files. A RAW file has a format that is tailored to suit the sensor on the particular camera that produced it. There are not only differences from one manufacturer to another, but even the cameras from a given maker have different RAW formats. This is not a major problem with the Adobe Camera RAW add-on, as it can handle RAW files from a huge range of cameras. However, there can be a significant delay between a new camera being released and the Camera RAW add-on being updated to accommodate it. It might still be possible to load the unsupported RAW images into Photoshop via file conversion supplied with the camera, but in order to fully utilize RAW files with Photoshop it is necessary for them to be supported by the Camera RAW add-on.

Non-Destructive

Editing of RAW files is of the non-destructive variety. In other words, changes made to an image in the Camera RAW add-on do not alter the RAW file. This file is the raw data from the camera's sensor, and that is the way it stays. Non-destructive editing leaves the RAW file unchanged, and details of the editing are stored in a companion file when the changes are saved. Of course, when the file is opened in Photoshop it can be saved in the usual way in the normal range of output file types, and the normal way of operating applies.

You then have the original RAW file, a file containing the changes made using the Camera RAW add-on, and the file or files saved after editing the image in Photoshop. Once a RAW file is loaded into Photoshop it is not possible to save it in the original RAW format. Adobe's own RAW format (Photoshop RAW) is available as a file type when saving images, but this is not the same as the RAW format of the original image. A non-compressed format such as TIFF must be used when saving RAW images if the full quality of the original image is to be retained.

It is normally important to keep copies of unedited images stored away safely somewhere where they will not be accidentally edited and irreversibly changed. This is less important with RAW images because any editing of them will not change the RAW file. In order to go back to the original image it is merely necessary to copy the image file to another folder. The companion file containing the editing details should not be copied. Loading the copied file into Camera RAW will take things "back to square one", and the loaded image will be free of any editing previously applied to it, no matter how many changes were made. Of course, it is

Fig.4.1 Opening a RAW file produces a new editing window

still advisable to have backup copies of your image files stored on another disc drive in case the main hard drive becomes faulty and the data on it is lost.

Opening

Opening a RAW file in Photoshop results in a new editing window appearing (Figure 4.1). This is effectively a photo editing program in its own right, and many of Photoshop's main editing facilities are available from the Camera RAW editor. The new window will probably be quite small at its default size, but it can be resized in the normal way by dragging the sides and corners. It is advisable to make it as large as possible, or very nearly so. Note that there are no Minimise, Restore Down, or Close buttons in the top right-hand corner of the window, so dragging is the only way of resizing it.

Before you start using the editor it is important to understand the operation of the three buttons near the bottom right-hand corner of the window. The Cancel button operates in the normal fashion, and using it therefore closes the window and any changes made to the image are not saved. Done is effectively a Save button, and using this one closes the window and saves the changes. Of course, the RAW file remains unchanged, and it is actually another file with details of the changes that is saved to disc. Provided you keep the RAW file and its companion editing file

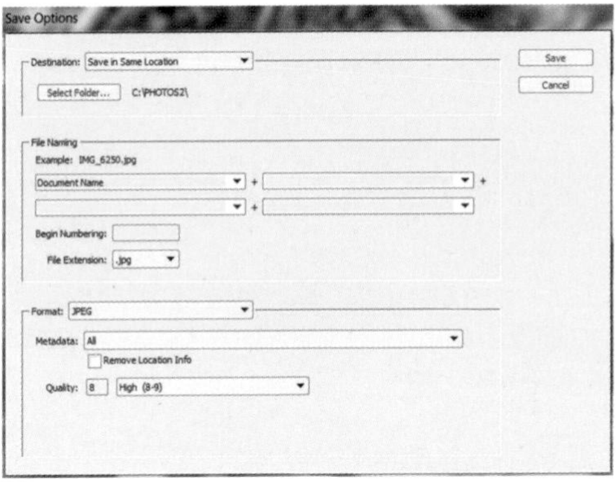

Fig.4.2 Files can be saved in various formats

together in the same folder, opening the RAW file again will result in the edited version being displayed. The editing file has the same name as the RAW file, but with a different extension such as XMP.

Using the Open Image button is the same as the Done type, but it additionally opens the edited image in Photoshop. It is then a normal Photoshop image that can be edited further and saved in any of the supported image formats. As pointed out previously, changes made in Photoshop will not alter the RAW file or its companion editing file as it is not possible to save the image in its original RAW format. Once loaded into Photoshop, any changes have to be saved in one of the normal image file formats such as PSD, JPEG, or TIFF.

It is possible to save images in Photoshop (PSD), JPEG, TIFF and digital negative (DNG) formats from within the Camera RAW add-on. Operating the Save Image button near the bottom left-hand corner of the window brings up the dialogue box of Figure 4.2, where things such as the required file format, destination folder, and image quality are selected. Note that the dialogue box will change to suit the file format selected, and that only the relevant options for that format will be displayed.

RAW editor

The editor displays the loaded image in the main panel on the left, and a range of tools are provided in the toolbar above the image. These include the panning (hand) tool, which is used in conjunction with the zoom tool, and the zoom menu and buttons near the bottom left corner of the image panel. There are other tools such as basic rotation types, red-eye reduction, crop and straighten tools.

A range of controls are provided in the panel on the right. There are ten buttons towards the top of the panel on the right, just below the histogram.

These provide access to ten different versions of the control panel, and they effectively act as tabs. The default version of the control panel has a useful range of controls that cover brightness, colour saturation, and so on.

It is not essential to make any changes to a RAW file before loading it into Photoshop, and there may be no point in doing so if all the basics seem to be correct. It can be loaded into Photoshop, and any "fine tuning" can be carried out, and then it can be printed, saved in the required format, or whatever. On the other hand, if there is clearly a problem with the colour balance or exposure, it is best to correct the problem as accurately as possible before loading the image into Photoshop.

The histogram can be useful when making adjustments to the brightness, contrast, and colour balance, but to a large extent you have to trust your own judgement and adjust things "by eye". The White Balance menu offers a range of preset types, including an Auto option. This is much the same as the options offered by most digital cameras, and like the white balance settings of a camera, it might or might not give the desired result. If none of the preset white balance settings "fit the bill", use the one that gives the best results or select the As Shot option, and then use the two slider controls to set the white balance manually. Vibrance and Saturation controls are available near the bottom of the control panel.

Clarifying Clarity

There is also a Clarity control in this section of the control panel, and this has no real equivalent in Photoshop. The image will become "softer" if you adjust it to the left, or sharper if this slider is set towards the right. It is a bit like a sharpening control with a large radius setting, but it can also be used to blur an image. It does not seem to be quite as simple as that though, and the way in which it operates is sometimes likened to the Vibrance control. It provides an increase or decrease in local contrast, but it has more effect in the mid tones and areas of low contrast than it does in areas that already have high contrast.

The purpose of this control is to increase the "depth" of an image, or decrease it. By all means use this control if you like the effect it provides, but I suspect that most Camera RAW users simply ignore it. It should not be regarded as an alternative to the sharpening controls, which are a much better option if sharpening is required.

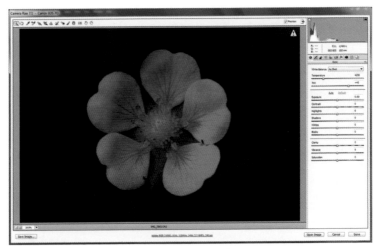

Fig.4.3 This photograph is underexposed by two stops

Brightness/Contrast

The six controls in the middle section of the control panel enable the contrast and brightness to be adjusted. The Exposure control enables the picture to be brightened or darkened to correct exposure errors. As always with this type of thing, noise can be a problem if a heavily underexposed photograph is lightened, and only a limited amount of detail might be recovered from the gloom. An overexposed photograph can be darkened, but this might leave a lack of detail in burned-out highlights. When working with a RAW file you can at least recover any detail that was recorded by the camera, and are not hampered by anything that was lost when the camera converted the RAW data to a JPEG file.

In the example of Figure 4.3 I have deliberately underexposed the photograph by two stops, and it is obviously far too dark. In Figure 4.4 I have used the Exposure control to increase the exposure by two stops, and I have then made some adjustments to the contrast and colour balance. Finally, sharpening was added, but no noise reduction of any kind was used. I have perhaps overdone the contrast and the sharpening, and considering the poor technical quality of the original it has come up quite well, but lifting some detail from the virtually black background has produced a very grainy end result. While it is often possible to get passable results from underexposed or overexposed RAW images, it is

Fig.4.4 Using the exposure control has greatly improved the image

much better if you can get the exposure fairly accurate in the first place so that only minor adjustments are needed later.

There are Shadow and Highlight controls that operate in a similar fashion to their Photoshop equivalents, but their adjustment range is more limited, and they have the ability to lighten or darken their part of the tone range. The Whites control can move the maximum light levels up or down while leaving the lowest levels unchanged. The range of tones is stretched or compressed from the high end, and this effect is clearly visible if you watch the histogram while adjusting this control. The Blacks control is similar, but it stretches/compresses the light levels from the low end, leaving the highest levels unaltered.

These controls can be used to ensure that the whites are genuinely white, and that the blacks are genuinely black. There are clipping indicators in the top left and right-hand corners of the histogram, and these go white when clipping of all three colour channels is achieved at their respective ends of the tone range. Using these controls you can deliberately

Fig.4.5 The Auto option has not worked well in this case

introduce a certain amount of clipping at high and (or) low levels, or set something less than the full tone range.   In most cases there would probably be no point in doing so, but suppose an object is photographed against a black background, that actually turns out to be something less

Fig.4.6 A simplified Curves facility is available

than uniformly black in the photograph. Provided the highest levels in the background are something close to fully black, setting them as such using the Blacks control would remove the blotchiness but would not significantly degrade other parts of the image.

There are two links near the top of the control panel, which operate as buttons. The Default one just resets all the controls to their original settings, and provides an easy means of getting back to "square one" if you make a complete mess of things. The Camera RAW add-on is primarily a means of making manual adjustments, but the Auto link enables the brightness, contrast, and white balance to be set automatically. As with any automatic facility of this type, it does not always work particularly well. In the example of Figure 4.5 it has "bleached" the lighter parts of the picture and made matters worse rather than better.

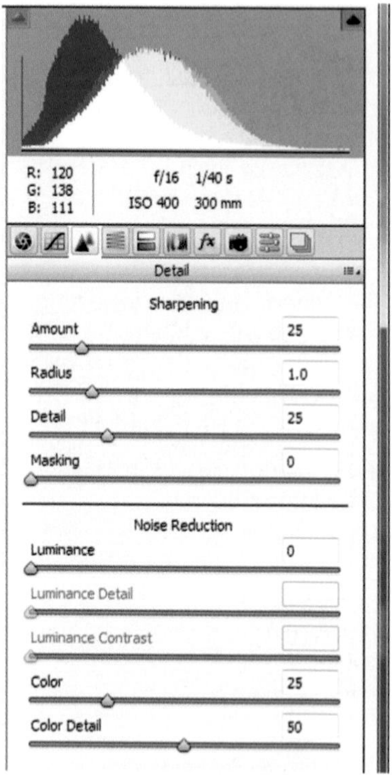

Fig.4.7 Sharpening and noise reduction facilities are available

A wide range of additional facilities are available via the other buttons near the top of the control panel. A simplified but useful version of the Photoshop Curves facility is available for example (Figure 4.6). There are further sections for correcting lens distortions, and for sharpening and noise reduction (Figure 4.7). It is not essential to make use of these since they largely duplicate facilities that are available from within Photoshop, and they probably have no advantage over using the Photoshop equivalents. My preference is definitely to get the brightness, contrast and white balance correct and then load the image into Photoshop for any further editing. As far as I can ascertain, there is no Print facility in the Camera RAW add-on, so it is necessary to load images into Photoshop in order to produce prints.

Camera RAW and JPEG

It is actually possible to open a JPEG file in the Camera RAW add-on, and its range of controls can then be used to edit the image. On the face of it there is no point in doing so, but it is worth considering if you prefer an aspect of the Camera RAW facility such as its way of handling luminance and white balance adjustments, or its simplified but effective version of the Curves facility.

A JPEG file is opened in the Camera RAW add-on by first launching Photoshop, and then selecting Open As from the File menu. This produces the usual file/folder browser which is used to select the required image file. Select Camera RAW from the Open As menu, and then open the file. This will produce the Camera RAW program, complete with the opened JPEG file (Figure 4.8).

The required changes are then made to the image, after which it can be loaded into Photoshop using the Open Image button. The image can then be edited further if required, after which it is saved in the usual way. Alternatively, it can be edited using the Camera RAW facility and then saved directly via the Save Image button. The four usual image formats are available. Of course, it is a JPEG file that is being edited and not a true RAW file, and non-destructive editing is not possible. Using the Done button simply abandons any changes made to the image. The source JPEG file is not altered, and no changes to the image are saved.

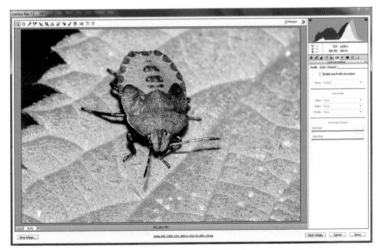

Fig.4.8 A JPEG image can be opened in the Camera RAW add-on

Index